Noemi Steuer, Michelle Engeler, Elísio Macamo (eds.)
Dealing with Elusive Futures

**Culture and Social Practice**

NOEMI STEUER, MICHELLE ENGELER, ELÍSIO MACAMO (EDS.)
**Dealing with Elusive Futures**
University Graduates in Urban Africa

[transcript]

Published with the support of the Swiss National Science Foundation.

FONDS NATIONAL SUISSE
SCHWEIZERISCHER NATIONALFONDS
FONDO NAZIONALE SVIZZERO
SWISS NATIONAL SCIENCE FOUNDATION

**Bibliographic information published by the Deutsche Nationalbibliothek**
The Deutsche Nationalbibliothek lists this publication in the Deutsche Nationalbibliografie; detailed bibliographic data are available in the Internet at http://dnb.d-nb.de

© 2017 transcript Verlag, Bielefeld

All rights reserved. No part of this book may be reprinted or reproduced or utilized in any form or by any electronic, mechanical, or other means, now known or hereafter invented, including photocopying and recording, or in any information storage or retrieval system, without permission in writing from the publisher.

Cover layout: Kordula Röckenhaus, Bielefeld
Cover illustration: Fanta Diarra, Bamako 2015
Printed and bound in Great Britain by Marston Book Services Ltd, Oxfordshire
Print-ISBN 978-3-8376-3949-0
PDF-ISBN 978-3-8394-3949-4

# Table of contents

**Context | 7**

**1 Elusive Futures**
An Introduction
*Michelle Engeler & Noemi Steuer* | 9

**2 Negotiating the Future**
Young Graduates Respond to Career Uncertainty in Tanzania
*Richard Faustine Sambaiga* | 29

**3 Ça va aller**
The Role of Hope in Burkinabe University Graduates' Navigation towards the Future
*Maike Birzle* | 53

**4 ›Opening up *La Chance*‹**
(Un)certainty among University Graduates in Bamako, Mali
*Susann Ludwig* | 69

**5 Looking for Better Opportunities**
An Analysis of Guinean Graduates' Agency
*Carole Ammann* | 93

**6 Politics of the Future – Riots of the Now**
Temporal Horizons of Youth in Upheavals in England and Guinea
*Joschka Philipps* | 123

**7 Managing Uncertainty**
Youth Unemployment, Responsibilisation and Entrepreneurship
Training Programmes in Ethiopia
*Julian Tadesse* | 147

**8 Epilogue**
Uncertainty and Elusive Futures
*Elísio Macamo* | 179

**On the Authors** | 195

# Context

The authors of this book met for the first time in 2014 at the Conference of the African Studies Associations in Germany (VAD) in the context of the panel ›Elusive Futures: Time and Uncertainty in the Career Practices of Young African Graduates‹, organised by Dr Noemi Steuer and Dr Michelle Engeler. Additional writing workshops and discussions have led to the various chapters in this volume. The research project ›Construire son Avenir‹, headed by Prof. Elísio Macamo and based at the Centre for African Studies Basel of the University Basel in Switzerland, served as our substantial point of departure; the project accompanied young men and women in urban Burkina Faso and Mali and explored their career practices and future planning after graduating from university. This project owes a substantial debt to Dr Claudia Roth who, together with Noemi Steuer, developed its initial idea and research approach. Dr Roth sadly passed away in 2012 following a long period of illness. ›Dealing with Elusive Futures‹ thus forms part of her scientific heritage, and we gratefully continue to be inspired by her reflections and writings.

The organisation of the edited volume was complemented by the scientific communication project ›Longing for the Future‹, headed and coordinated by Dr Noemi Steuer and Dr Michelle Engeler. In that project, research data on young people and their handling of the future in both Africa and Europe were visualised and interpreted through various artistic projects that included photography exhibitions, theatre performances and interactive audio walks in Bamako, Basel and Ouagadougou. It is in this context that the pictures integrated in the edited volume ›Dealing with Elusive Futures‹ were developed; inspired by the life trajectories of young West African graduates, photo students from the *Cadre de Promotion pour la Formation en Photographie* (CFP, Bamako, Mali) were called upon to reflect on the experiences and perspectives of young people and their transition to adulthood. The photographs contained in this book are examples drawn from that visual art work and reflection.

All in all, the edited volume ›Dealing with Elusive Futures‹ is the result of numerous examinations and encounters and, accordingly, provides not only scientific and visual insights but also opens up different views and informs new questions in the broader context of conducting research on being young and, as we argue, doing adulthood in and beyond urban Africa.

## Acknowledgements

The Swiss National Science Foundation SNSF generously funded the research activities that made the publication of this edited volume possible. In addition, the editors wish to thank transcript Verlag for their work and support, and Steven Parham for the careful language editing.

# 1 Elusive Futures
## An Introduction

*Michelle Engeler & Noemi Steuer*

This volume and its introduction take a closer look at young graduates and their hopes and life plans for the future. In our endeavour we address two research challenges: first, the challenge of doing research on youth and the future; and second, the challenge of examining young graduates' imaginations and hopes for a time that is yet to come.

It stands to reason that the future can be thought of as a land of pure possibility made of hopes and promises. While individuals strive to conquer, chart and assess this land, its shape lies beyond their grasp. At the same time, though, the time yet to come steers our actions and endeavours at various levels as a pervasive reference system. In spite of this all-embracing relevance, every excursion into the realm of the future – be it through day-dreaming, fortune-telling or through calculations made by experts – can never fail to remind us of the elusive nature of the future. Our volume addresses this intrinsic feature of the future from the two different angles derived from the level of experience and from the level of methodology.

We aim to ask how actors who live in a very dynamic and unforeseeable context make plans and statements about the future or, even more to the point, how they can have a bearing on the time to come. Beyond this, we seek to discuss a methodological question pertaining to the extent to which the future can be made available to research. Since doing research on the future – even if this is on a future deeply embedded in, or in conjunction with, the present – is always a methodological challenge, the question arises how we can study something that is not tangible, something that evades our grasp and yet shapes the life of individuals.

To appreciate what it means to deal with the future empirically and methodologically, we draw on a distinction made by the French anthropologist Marc Augé concerning two ways of relating to it. According to him, a distinction is made between »one [way] which makes the future a successor to the past, the schematic one; and the other which makes it a birth, an inauguration« (Augé 2014: 4). The claim here is that the future becomes relevant to the social sciences to the extent that we can think of it primarily as the context within which processes that have a beginning will evolve and perhaps end and, second, as a set of structural features made available to researchers and actors through consequences. In other words, we retrieve time through positing structural factors which enable us to articulate individuals' actions within a temporal dimension. While the distinction between a schematic future and an inaugural future provides a useful vocabulary with which to describe the group of young graduates from the perspective of the concept of the future, it also brings to the fore the future's elusive nature.

We have taken a conscious decision to concentrate on young graduates in this volume, that is, on men and women who have pursued their education and ended up with a university degree. Upon their independence the new African nation-states expected their first locally-trained university graduates to inaugurate a new beginning for their countries. They were the new nations' hope for the future. The countries also nurtured them as the harbingers of development. The career paths of the generations of university graduates that followed fell into a schematic framework that saw the future as a logical repetition of the past as defined in the inaugural moment. This was the time of national »cadres«, i.e. of professionals who were being trained to operate the burgeoning machinery of the state.

This has changed radically in recent decades: from being a highly praised development elite, university graduates have become those often described as only waiting for adulthood (Honwana 2012). This has been mainly due to economic hardship and consequent unemployment, political crisis and related social tensions. In particular since the structural adjustment programmes of the 1980s, young graduates have no longer been able to take their future for granted (Mohamedbhai 2011). Neoliberal reforms and socio-political change have disrupted the patterns set by previous generations on how to become respected adults and constitute the elite of the country. This is the background against which the contributions in this volume must be read. Each chapter depicts various facets of contemporary young graduates and how they manage their everyday lives whilst moving towards the future. To illustrate this we have collected case studies from urban Burkina Faso, Ethiopia, Guinea, Mali and Tanzania.

The aim of these case studies is to advance the field of research on youth and the future in three main respects: first, they concentrate on young graduates' various contexts of action and thereby seek to show how to make the future available for social scientific research. Second, they help to further understand an often understudied aspect of African youth: the context of well-educated young men and women. Finally, they shed new light on being young and growing up in and beyond urban Africa.

It is against this background that we argue that our case studies demonstrate that young graduates are not only »being young«, that is, living and struggling in the present; they are in fact also constantly »doing something« in regard to their social becoming – not only after, but even before graduation. This perspective disagrees with studies which argue that young people these days struggle to become respected adults. We argue that this is not the case, and that they are actually already doing adulthood in different spheres of social life: they may do internships, care for their own children, pursue their studies, dream of marrying, join youth movements or political parties, or simply meet friends with whom to discuss while drinking tea.

The following sections of this introduction elaborate upon this perspective and provide insight into the contributions that make up this edited volume.

## RESEARCHING THE FUTURE

The current importance of the question of how society comes to terms with the future is reflected in an increasing number of publications in the social sciences and humanities. For a long time, however, social scientists dealt with the topic only peripherally and preferred to study the past or, especially related to the methods of social anthropology, the here and the now. Even when studies concerned themselves with this category, the future was often perceived as a normative trajectory with teleological aspects well exemplified through the concepts of progress and development (Goldstone and Obarrio 2016b: 12). Numerous scholars have now expressed the need to finally complement the classic past- and present-oriented focus by including research on the relations of the present and the future (Crapanzano 2004; Goldstone and Obarrio 2016a; Munn 1992; Pelican and Heiss 2014). These authors have also hinted that notions of the future are deeply embedded in the concepts of time of the respective societies. This actually makes the future very relevant for social anthropology and related fields of study (Appadurai 2004; Mische 2009).

In brief, socio-anthropological contributions have centred on two distinct approaches, both of which are characterised by actor-centred perspectives. One approach focuses primarily on social actions that contain future orientations, i.e. aspirations (Appadurai 2004), imaginations (Crapanzano 2004), hope (Turner 2015) or plans and dreams (Nilsen 1999). The second approach has discussed more how actors experience and deal with the inherent uncertainties of the future, mainly referring to uncertain terrains due to political turbulence or economic crisis (Vigh 2006). Whereas the search for certainty and control has been highlighted in the context of risk and illness (Jenkins 2005: 10; Whyte 2009: 214), the important volume ›Ethnographies of Uncertainty in Africa‹ by Elisabeth Cooper and David Pratten adopts another perspective by examining the brighter side of uncertainty (2015). Drawing on the work of John Dewey and his philosophy of pragmatism, the authors frame uncertainty in a productive way as a motor for innovation and creation (Cooper and Pratten 2015: 13).

Broadly speaking, social scientists who discuss the future in the context of youth and uncertainty rarely address methodological challenges beyond simply stating that such challenges indeed exist. Jennifer Johnson-Hanks and her research on uncertainty and intentional action in the context of young, educated Cameroonian women is an exception in this respect (Johnson-Hanks 2005). In her research she asked young women about their plans for the future, especially in regard to having children. Instead of receiving precise answers she was told by her informants, rather vaguely, that they cannot make plans because they do not know the future (Johnson-Hanks 2005: 367). Johnson-Hanks described this attitude as »judicious opportunism«, that is, a response to the volatility of life in an extremely uncertain context. She argues that, due to the contingent offers of life, what works best is the most flexible strategy »that keeps every alternative open as long as possible, and that permits the actor to act rapidly and flexibly to take advantage of whatever opportunities arise« (Johnson-Hanks 2005: 483).

Based on her fruitful insight, we would like to go a step further by focusing on the intrinsic feature of social action. This leads us to the work of Alfred Schütz and Thomas Luckman (Schütz and Luckman 2003). Their phenomenologically-grounded analysis of action proffers revealing observations about the core of human action and can provide a different approach for methodologically grasping hold of the uncertain future (Schütz and Luckmann 2003: 467ff). By developing the concept of the »project« as the fundamental meaning of every action, they show that action itself entails the element of »projectivity« coupled with inherent uncertainty while at the same time enabling further actions. Thus, acting in the present not only immanently carries the future but also guarantees the ability to act in the future. In other words, human agency is always in preparation of further action (see Macamo 2017: 4f). Methodologically speaking, we can retrieve the future by articulating it with social action in the present. Individuals tame the future in the present by investing their energy into enabling action – or, in the words of Pelican and Heiss, by »making the future« (Pelican and Heiss 2014: 7). Even if contexts of uncertainty may compel actors to refrain from developing future plans, they still act in order to be able to act and, thereby, they offer insight into how they create future opportunities (Macamo 2008). Expanding upon Johnson-Hanks' approach, we argue methodologically that social action is always in the process of becoming and, for this reason, requires an open-ended approach to study the ongoing unfolding of very different futures, especially in rapidly shifting and precarious contexts. Like this we also follow the objectives of Goldstone and Obarrio and illuminate »the plurality of routes through which African futures are being engendered and apprehended« (Goldstone and Obarrio 2016b: 4).

## YOUTH AND AFRICAN UNIVERSITY GRADUATES

There is no shortage of research on youth, and reviewing it would certainly go beyond the scope of this introduction. Many authors also contextualise youth in relation to time, either by describing young people as a vanguard or by perceiving them as still waiting for the time yet to come. However, many contributions that address young people living in

Africa do not consciously address university graduates. Studies that at least discuss higher education more broadly have a tendency to focus on questions related to development and/or funding (see e.g. Oketch 2016). Those works that focus on the people shaping the universities very often place the student body at the centre of attention and discuss student activism and protests (for a recent example, see Luescher et al. 2016). Both topics are notably discussed in the context of South Africa. Social anthropological contributions that discuss the lives of students or, like us, depict young graduates' everyday life and plans for the future in other sub-Saharan African nations are largely absent. Exceptions include the many insightful publications by Mazzocchetti, who in particular discusses students and young graduates in Burkina Faso (Mazzocchetti 2006; Mazzocchetti 2009; Mazzocchetti 2014). Furthermore, a small number of historical examinations provide us with crucial background information on the making of local universities and their key figures (see for instance the writings of Andreas Eckert (2000; 2004; 2006) or Andrea Behrends and Carola Lentz [2012]). These studies remind us that in many African countries following independence, a university diploma from one of the national universities guaranteed a life of prosperity and social recognition: predominantly, these historical studies describe the students of newly established – or newly independent – institutions of higher education as future national elites, who upon graduation would work for the state administration. Accordingly, students and graduates are described as key economic and political representatives (Lentz 2009).

However, economic crises and related socio-political transformation processes and reforms since the 1980s have had a huge impact on youth and young graduates. University diplomas no longer guarantee a career and related social and/or class mobility (Mkandawire 1995; Mohamedbhai 2011). Thus, present-day students in urban sub-Saharan Africa often enjoy a precarious social status compared to the former elitist prestige of graduates, who could usually expect some degree of financial security and social exclusivity (Behrends and Lentz 2012; Behrends and Pauli 2012). Nevertheless, many youths in West Africa still think it is crucial to study, and having a university diploma continues to carry the hope of entrance into working life and adulthood. It is in this way that young men and women also try to escape local universities in the hope that a diploma from abroad is more valuable than one from local state universities (Efionayi-Mäder and Piguet 2014; Mazzocchetti 2014; Piguet 2013).

This edited volume, however, discusses those students who finally graduate from one of the local public universities. In all likelihood they have spent one or two terms elsewhere, or they dream of receiving an additional diploma from abroad – but all the authors contained in this edited volume talked to young graduates in those countries in which they actually graduated. Thus, the contributions here are based on extensive fieldwork conducted in the urban centres of Burkina Faso, Ethiopia, Guinea, Mali and Tanzania.

A more general look at scholarly literature discussing youth in the social sciences reveals that »youth« is generally understood as a social category rather than as a specific age group (Durham 2004). It follows that the time and place in which an individual considers themselves to be a youth, or is regarded as youth, is both situational and contested (Durham 2009: 723). In other words youth represents a category that is always in the process of being re-made in socio-political practices. Depending on the situation and the relations involved, the same person can be regarded as a child, a youth or an adult simultaneously (Christiansen et al. 2006: 12). Nevertheless, a number of publications consciously or unconsciously relate the topic of youth to time and the future (Martin et al. 2016). From a life-course perspective this makes perfect sense, for young people stand only at the very beginning of their trajectories and all the world yet lies ahead of them. Consequently, youth is often perceived as the future of a society or nation-state. It is against this background that some studies have conducted research on youth by relating the topic to the broader context of political change. Accordingly, titles of contributions situate youths between »vanguard and vandals« (Abbink and Van Kessel 2005) or between »rebels and patriots« (Rompel 2008), thus discussing young people and their potential for becoming actors for political change.

Aside from studies interested in politics and political transformation processes, there do exist studies which approach youth as both »social being« and »social becoming« and thereby regard being young as a condition that is inherently future-oriented, not least because it is assumed that young people's aim is to become socially accepted adults in the (near) future (Christiansen et al. 2006: 11). A prominent example of such an approach within African Studies are Henrik Vigh's reflections on »social navigation« (Christiansen et al. 2006; Vigh 2009). He uses the concept of social navigation as an analytical tool to shed light on the way in which young people in Guinea-Bissau come of age and guide their lives through complex socio-political circumstances. In fact, these complex circumstances induce various authors to situate young people in what Helga Nowotny calls an »extended present« (Nowotny 1988). In other words, planning the future – or coming of age – becomes all but impossible due to political crisis and also because of joblessness and a related excess of time in the present. It is in this connection that Alcinda Honwana describes youth in Africa as the »waithood generation«. She argues that the majority are not able to obtain work and hence to achieve the attributes of adulthood such as being economically independent, getting married and having children (Honwana 2012: 3). In other words, young people are described as being trapped in the here and now, as having an »excess of time« (Brannen and Nilsen 2002), or as willingly remaining in the present because they no longer trust the future.

Based on our research on young graduates we have developed a different perspective on these matters, and we argue that the contexts of action within which individuals engage can unfold and render visible the temporal dimension we seek. In this sense, we take the way in which young graduates manage their daily life and imagine their future not only to be representative of »being young« in the here and now, but also to be constantly »doing adulthood« in various spheres of their lives.

We will now briefly discuss the various contributions to this volume in order to illustrate critical aspects of our perspective on youth as well as to show how our case studies represent a way to methodologically grasp young graduates' plans, hopes and expectations through looking at social action in the present.

## DIFFERENT DIMENSIONS OF FUTURE-CREATING ACTIVITIES

The book chapters of this edited volume depict different regional backgrounds in urban sub-Saharan Africa and include case studies from Burkina Faso, Ethiopia, Guinea, Mali and Tanzania. All of them focus on youth and their various future-creating activities. Generally speaking, these activities, ideas and goals are constantly adjusted to the actors' changing contexts and actions, and they exhibit a high degree of shifting and dynamism. This leads to meandering life trajectories, and at times the initial designations made by the respective researchers can no longer be recognised. The authors thereby show how both goals as well as the trajectories that lead to them relate to individual wishes but also follow social ideas or collective plans and utopias. In all cases imaginations of the future differ from the experienced here-and-now and reveal a striving for improvement.

From a substantive point of view, the critical situation on the labour market is one of the prominent features with which all young graduates portrayed in this volume have to grapple. And, although most graduates perceive (university) diplomas as the key to a better life, they also know that reality is often much more complex. Finding appropriate employment is far from being guaranteed by having higher education and corresponding degrees. In essence there are only rarely straight paths which lead to desired professional activities; in most cases graduates have to deal with circuitous ways and non-permanent appointments, often within different domains than the ones they wished for or for which they were educated, and often with very low or no remuneration at all. Such constraints quickly lead to decreased economic and social independence. Scientific discourse often describes this condition as »limbo life« or as corresponding to being stuck or as only waiting for adulthood (Honwana 2012; Masquelier 2005; Sommers 2012). The vocabulary used in this context often implies a type of passivity or resignation which, incidentally, may even hold true in some instances. It is more likely, however, that »passivity« or »resignation« are manifest functions of latent structures thoroughly grounded in actual things that young people do to come to terms with their circumstances.

The authors of this volume adopt a different perspective by showing how young graduates are busy with numerous activities and juggle a multitude of engagements. They also assume a panoply of roles by being parents, entrepreneurs and members of political movements or religious congregations – very often several of them at the same time. And despite the discrepancy between professional expectations and the lack of opportunities, one rarely finds expressions of living in liminal stages in their narratives. It goes without saying that our contributors also learnt about periods of despair and tiredness, but they also recognised »alternative pathways« (Carling 2015: 3) which represent a repertoire of conceivable strategies leading out of waithood.

The chapters written by Richard Sambaiga, Maike Birzle and Susann Ludwig all depict the issue of young graduates and their taming of an uncertain future by pointing to individual strategies and horizons. Richard Sambaiga's contribution provides a vivid picture of the diversity of individual career orientations of final-year students and young graduates from the Department of Sociology at the University of Dar es Salaam, Tanzania. Based on life histories and inspired by the theoretical reflections on agency by Emirbayer and Mische (1998), Sambaiga argues that young graduates are not reduced to mere victims of graduate unemployment, but instead are social actors who actively engage with their uncertain futures before and after graduating. Against this background, he argues that graduation can be described as a vital conjuncture during which young people are particularly oriented towards their future, a fact which allows him to research their projective actions as part of general human agency. He further discusses the challenge of young people's lived experiences in the present and their hoped-for or imagined futures, and he perceives the latter as a crucial marker for what finally takes place in the present.

An important issue that irrupts into Sambaiga's essay without being explicitly mentioned (other than as an inner disposition for managing the wide range of activities) is that of hope. In contrast to the extended research done by Daniel Mains (Mains 2012), where young men in urban Ethiopia are depicted as both possessing unprecedented aspirations and remaining without hope to realise them, Maike Birzle also highlights the important role of hope as a driving force to navigate the meandering pathways into the future. Not concrete career activities are at stake here but rather an inner attitude that allows individuals to keep up an emotional and future-directed orientation. Her analysis focuses on the phrase *ça va aller* – an expression that appeared repeatedly in the qualitative interviews she conducted with university graduates in Ouagadougou, the capital city of Burkina Faso. To exemplify her argument, amongst other things Birzle hints at the annual recruitment tests for the civil service, which most of her informants perceive as the likeliest way to enter the job market. Despite the fact that only a small percentage of them will finally win the *concours*, they continue to hope for the best. Part of hoping is thereby also to live off one's faith by praying regularly, fasting and attending church or mosque services. Here, hope is not only an abstract idea but essentially informs young graduates' practices in continuously and optimistically navigating the uncertain terrain of the present.

In her contribution Susann Ludwig also reflects on young graduates' motivations to hopefully »become someone«. She concentrates on narratives of individual and common experiences of Malian graduates and offers a typology of a phenomenon that inspires their minds as well as their practices: *la chance* – an emic concept with a wide semantic range pointing to that extraordinary moment of fulfilment when timing, place and action come together and provide an outlook which is completely different from the one imagined up to that point in time. In this respect, *la chance* fuses opportunity with destiny, and luck with serendipity. Based on the application of ethnomethodology's membership categorisation analysis to narrative interviews, Ludwig presents three types of *la chance*: prerequisites, sprouts and outcomes. She argues that these types are connected through practices of ›opening up *la chance*‹ – a process that consists of ›looking for‹, ›finding‹ and ›working with‹ *la chance*. In a context of high unemployment rates amongst university graduates, Ludwig explains, the phenomenon of *la chance* gains special significance because it offers a space for individual agency and, therefore, a bearing on the time to come. Even if *la chance* does not answer the question of why some academic peers succeed in creating a future while others do not, it does create a horizon of hope for everyone – and instead of waiting for miracles, they prepare the soil so that theses miracles might happen to them. In other words, it is the young graduates' conviction that *la chance* exists which creates a difference to the lived-in present.

These three insights show that the creational processes of an individually conceived future are always merged in certain ways with social commitments and thereby incorporate both individual and social horizons: »The future, even when it concerns the individual, always has a social dimension: it depends on others. [...] It is sometimes said that the individual ›constructs‹ his future, but others participate in that enterprise which is primarily a manifestation of social life« (Augé 2014: 2f). In Carole Ammann's paper the social dimension of the future gains special emphasis. Her gender-sensitive approach documents the interwoven layers and the diversity of young graduates' agency and their flexibility in the search for their hoped-for future. Drawing on the case study of Djénabou, a young intellectual woman living in Kankan, Guinea, Ammann illustrates that faith in God and having great respect for one's parents crucially informs the everyday practices of young students. Djénabou herself pursues high career ambitions and at the same time holds the desire to get married to a loving husband of her own choice – both of which are rather unusual aspirations for a young woman in Kankan. But by creating an irreproachable reputation in the eyes of her community as a »good young Muslim woman« who follows the existing gender and religious norms, Djénabou succeeds in carving out a way into her imagined future. Hence, gaining the confidence of her social environment enables Djénabou to explore new avenues and at the same time broadens the gendered, prescribed way towards independence.

The implication of others in the construction of future times achieves a different dimension when these »others« all band together to collectively pursue the same vision. Mostly approached within an institutional frame, collective ideas aspire to a future in an inaugural sense, in other words as a break with the past. A prominent topic in the available literature is that of young people and their potential to become actors for political change. Joschka Philipps' chapter analyses interviews and conversations with young men who were directly involved in popular upheavals in England and Guinea. By including a comparative perspective, the aim of his contribution is to ask how these young men – a group that also includes young graduates – talk about and shape the future through their political actions. Interestingly, he sees reason to believe that rioting youth from the urban margins in England seem to have been more excluded from politics than their counterparts in Guinea. These contrasting perspectives on the political future could be understood as being contingent upon whether people see politics as fixed and separate from them, or as evolving and open to manipulation, Philipps concludes. Where the political system is seen as stable and inaccessible, political exclusion may seem more definitive, whilst in contexts where exclusion is less clear-cut and politics more a matter of networks, the political future is likelier to appear as malleable and accessible to interference.

The last chapter in our book adopts a rather different perspective on the taming of future uncertainties. Julian Tadesse's case study is concerned with the role of the state in the context of the career trajectories of young graduates – and youths in general – in Ethiopia. By depicting state-funded entrepreneurship training programmes and their discursive context, he argues that the ruling regime has to be considered as a crucial factor in understanding young graduates' practices and manoeuvrings, not least because these programmes have recently become one of the Ethiopian government's favoured instruments in tackling youth unemployment. Tadesse argues that a largely structural problem – that of unemployment – is transformed into a question of individual attitude; and that this shifts the moral responsibility for economic insecurity onto young graduates. Moreover, uncertainties that accompany the establishing of a business are shown in a more positive light by pointing to the ›liberating‹ aspects of entrepreneurship. In this way the government simply tries to create entrepreneurial subjects in line with its developmental ideology. Structural problems such as access to finance, bureaucratic hurdles and the general problem of the education system not matching the needs of industry are toned down.

## SOCIAL BECOMING – DOING ADULTHOOD

We began our introduction by reflecting on how we can make the future available to the social sciences, and we proceeded to take a critical look at research conducted in the context of youths and their future planning. We have found that many publications describe young people's coming of age and their imaginations of the future or their being lost in the present, yet the majority of studies ignore young graduates and their future planning. Our assumption is that this omission is due to the methodological challenge posed by researching phenomena that entail a temporal dimension which has not yet been made concrete by social action. Our suggestion is that adopting a theoretical perspective that posits social action as enabling (see Macamo in this volume) retrieves the future for analysis. Social action in the present amounts to the construction of the future, but this future is one that does not necessarily respond to one's plans. This future is a contingent outcome of social action today.

This is the background against which qualifying the future as elusive appeared reasonable to us. The future is elusive because it always has the potential to turn out differently. This makes intuitive sense since in social settings with low degrees of predictability it remains difficult to institutionally secure the future outcomes of actions. The future is also elusive in the sense that it seems to slip away from the empirical grasp of researchers. It announces itself while at the same time appearing to refuse to be seized. What may appear to be the future today on the basis of today's social action, may recede into the background tomorrow as a result of what happened today.

We argue that this focus offers important new insight into the topic of being young and socially growing up, both in Africa and beyond. This can be exemplified by studying the education-to-work transition described in some of our chapters. The depicted realities show that many students are already engaged in working activities before they graduate or that they are at least looking for work. This suggests that it is an empirical question whether the period after graduation from university can be labelled as »transition«. In its literal sense transition means »going across«, a shifting from one condition to another; but this requires a period of stability and continuity before and after shifting. The situations of young graduates depicted in this volume instead remind us of a life in »permanent transition«. Thus, periods of stability and continuity may be inextricably entangled with transitional phases – not only while being a student and graduating, but also later in life. The future-oriented activities can thus be framed as a »social becoming« that is also relevant for adults or elders. There is a sense in which one could say that many of the portrayed young graduates are promoting their social becoming in different spheres; and this takes place both in the context of education and work as well as in social and family life, religion or politics. For this reason, it may not be accurate to frame them as young people only waiting for adulthood. Our perspective suggests that we are confronted with a new way of being and becoming somebody because young people tame the future by doing adulthood in different spheres of social life.

## Bibliography

Abbink, Jon, Ineke Van Kessel (eds.). 2005. *Vanguard or vandals. Youth, politics and conflict in Africa.* Leiden, Boston: Brill.

Appadurai, Arjun. 2004. »The Capacity to Aspire: Culture and the Terms of Recognition.« In *Culture and Public Action*, edited by V. Rao, M. Walton. Stanford: Stanford University Press. 59-84.

Augé, Marc. 2014. *The Future.* Translated by J. Howe. London, New York: Verso.

Behrends, Andrea, Carola Lentz. 2012. »Education, Careers, and Home Ties: The Ethnography of an Emerging Middle Class from Northern Ghana.« *Zeitschrift für Ethnologie* 137: 139-164.

Behrends, Andrea, Julia Pauli. 2012. »Zwischen Charisma und Korruption: Kontinuitäten und Brüche in der Auseinandersetzung mit Eliten in Afrika.« In *50 Jahre Unabhängigkeit in Afrika. Kontinuitäten, Brüche, Perspektiven*, edited by T. Bierschenk, E. Spies. Köln: Rüdiger Köppe Verlag. 301-320.

Brannen, Julia, Ann Nilsen. 2002. »Young People's Time Perspectives. From Youth to Adulthood.« *Sociology* 36(3): 513-537.

Christiansen, Catrine, Mats Utas, Henrik Vigh. 2006. »Navigating Youth, Generating Adulthood. Introduction.« In *Navigating Youth, Generating Adulthood. Social Becoming in an African Context*, edited by C. Christiansen, M. Utas, H. Vigh. Uppsala: Nordiska Afrikainstitutet. 9-28.

Cooper, Elizabeth, David Pratten. 2015. »Ethnographies of Uncertainty in Africa: An Introduction.« In *Ethnographies of Uncertainty in Africa*, edited by E. Cooper and D. Pratten. Basingstoke: Palgrave Macmillan. 1-16.

Crapanzano, Vincent. 2004. *Imaginative Horizons: An Essay in Literary-Philosophical Anthropology*. Chicago: University of Chicago Press.

Durham, Deborah. 2009. »Youth.« In *Encyclopedia of Social and Cultural Anthropology*, edited by A. Barnard, J. Spencer. London: Routledge. 722-723.

Durham, Deborah. 2004. »Disappearing Youth: Youth as a Social Shifter in Botswana.« *American Ethnologist* 34(4): 589-605.

Eckert, Andreas. 2006. »Panafrikanismus, afrikanische Intellektuelle und Europa im 19. und 20. Jahrhundert.« *Journal of Modern African Studies* 4(2): 224-240.

Eckert, Andreas. 2004. »Universitäten und die Politik des Exils. Afrikanische Studenten und anti-koloniale Politik in Europa, 1900-1960.« In *Universitäten und Kolonialismus*, edited by A. Eckert. Stuttgart: Franz Steiner Verlag. 129-145.

Eckert, Andreas. 2000. »Universitäten, Nationalismus und koloniale Herrschaft. Zur Vor- und Frühgeschichte der Hochschulen in Afrika 1860-1960.« In *Zwischen Wissens- und Verwaltungsökonomie. Zur Geschichte des Berliner Charité-Krankenhauses im 19. Jahrhundert*, edited by E.J. Engstrom, V. Hess. Stuttgart: Franz Steiner Verlag. 238-252.

Efionayi-Mäder, Denise, Etienne Piguet. 2014. »Western African Student Migration: A Response to the Globalisation of Knowledge.« In *Education, Learning, Training: Critical Issues for Development*, International Development Policy series No. 5, Geneva: Graduate Institute Publications, Boston: Brill-Nijhoff. 174-194.

Goldstone, Brian, Juan Obarrio (eds.). 2016a. *African Futures. Essays on Crisis, Emergence, and Possibility*. Chicago: University of Chicago Press.

Goldstone, Brian, Juan Obarrio (eds.). 2016b. »Introduction: Untimely Africa?« In *African Futures. Essays on Crisis, Emergence, and Possibili-*

*ty*, edited by B. Goldstone, J. Obarrio. Chicago: University of Chicago Press. 1-19.

Honwana, Alcinda. 2012. *The Time of Youth. Work, Social Change, and Politics in Africa*. Sterling: Kumarian Press.

Jenkins, Richard, Hanne Jessen, Stephen Vibeke. 2005. »Matters of Life and Death. The Control of Uncertainty and the Uncertainty of Control.« In *Managing Uncertainty. Ethnographic Studies of Illness, Risk and the Struggle for Control*, edited by R. Jenkins, H. Jessen, S. Vibeke. Copenhagen: Museum Tusculanum Press. 9-29.

Johnson-Hanks, Jennifer. 2005. »When the Future Decides. Uncertainty and Intentional Action in Contemporary Cameroon.« *Current Anthropology* 46(3): 363-385.

Lentz, Carola. 2009. »Constructing Ethnicity: Elite Biographies and Funerals in Ghana.« In *Ethnicity, Belonging and Biography*, edited by G. Rosenthal, A. Bogner. Berlin: Lit Verlag. 181-202.

Luescher, Thierry M., Manja Klemenčič, James Otieno Jowi (eds.). 2016. *Student Politics in Africa: Representation and Activism*. Oxford: African Minds.

Macamo, Elísio. 2008. »The Taming of Fate. Approaching Risk from a Social Action Perspective.« *Case Studies from Southern Mozambique*. Universität Bayreuth: Kulturwissenschaftliche Fakultät.

Mains, Daniel. 2012. *Hope is Cut. Youth, Unemployment, and the Future in Urban Ethiopia*. Philadelphia: Temple University Press.

Martin, Jeannett, Christian Ungruhe, Tabea Häberlein. 2016. »Young Future Africa. Images, Imaginations and Its Making: An Introduction.« *AnthropoChildren* 6(6): 1-18.

Mazzocchetti, Jacinthe. 2014. »›Le diplôme visa‹: entre mythe et mobilité. Imaginaries et migrations des étudiants et diplômés Burkinabè.« *Cahiers d'études africaines* LIV(1-2): 213-214.

Mazzocchetti, Jacinthe. 2009. Être étudiant à Ouagadougou. Imaginaire et précarité. Paris: Karthala.

Mazzocchetti, Jacinthe. 2006. »›Quand les poussins se réunissent, ils font peur à l'épervier...‹ Les étudiants burkinabè en politique.« *Politique Africaine* 101: 83-101.

Mische, Ann. 2009. »Projects and Possibilities. Researching Futures in Action.« *Sociological Forum* 24(3): 694-704.

Mkandawire, Thandika. 1995. »Three Generations of African Academics. A Note.« *Transformation* 28: 75-83.

Mohamedbhai, Goolam. 2011. »African Higher Education: The Rise and Fall in the 20th Century.« *International Higher Education* 62: 17-18.

Munn, Nancy D. 1992. »The Cultural Anthropology of Time: A Critical Essay.« *Annual Review of Anthropology* 21: 93-123.

Nilsen, Ann. 1999. »Where is the Future? Time and Space as Categories in Analyses of Young People's Images of the Future. Innovation.« *European Journal of Social Science Research* 12(2): 175-194.

Nowotny, Helga. 1988. »From the Future to the Extended Present.« In *The Formulation of Time Preferences in a Multidisciplinary Perspective*, edited by G. Kirsch, P. Nijkam, K. Zimmermann. Aldershot: Avebury. 17-31.

Oketch, Moses. 2016. »Financing Higher Education in sub-Saharan Africa: Some Reflections and Implications for Sustainable Development.« *Higher Education* 72(4): 525-539.

Pelican, Michaela, Jan Patrick Heiss. 2014. »›Making a Future‹ in Contemporary Africa. Introduction.« *Journal des Africanistes* 84(1): 7-19.

Piguet, Etienne. 2013. *The Move to Move. What motivates West African university students to consider leaving their countries*. Geneva: Swiss Network for International Studies (research report).

Rompel, Dörte. 2008. *Rebellen oder Patrioten? Jugend im politischen Prozess der Côte d'Ivoire von 1990 bis heute*. Frankfurt am Main: Brandes & Apsel.

Schütz, Alfred, Thomas Luckmann. 2003. *Strukturen der Lebenswelt*. Stuttgart: UTB.

Turner, Simon. 2015. »›We wait for miracles‹: Ideas of Hope and Future among Clandestine Burundian Refugees in Nairobi.« In *Ethnographies of Uncertainty in Africa*, edited by E. Cooper, D. Pratten. Basingstoke: Palgrave Macmillan. 173-191.

Vigh, Henrik. 2009. »Motion Squared. A Second Look at the Concept of Social Navigation.« *Anthropological Theory* 9(4): 419-438.

Vigh, Henrik. 2006. *Navigating Terrains of War. Youth and Soldiering in Guinea-Bissau*. Oxford, New York: Berghahn Books.

Whyte, Susan Reynolds. 2009. »Epilogue.« In *Dealing with Uncertainty in Contemporary African Lives*, edited by L. Haram, C. B. Yamba. Uppsala: Nordiska Afrikainstitutet. 213-216.

© Oumou Traoré

© Fatoumata Traoré

© Oumou Traoré

# 2 Negotiating the Future

Young Graduates Respond to Career Uncertainty in Tanzania

*Richard Faustine Sambaiga*

## INTRODUCTION

It is acknowledged that the ongoing social and political transformations in African countries have dramatically altered the contexts that structure career choices among young university graduates throughout the continent (Al-Samarrai and Bennell 2007; Johnson-Hanks 2002). With the few exceptions of graduates who pursue degree programmes for which the demand for graduates exceeds the supply of graduates to the labour market, a clear shift from career certainties to career uncertainties for young graduates is a reality in African countries like Tanzania (Mukyanuzi 2003; Emirbayer and Mische 1998). This contribution examines what it means for a young person to graduate in a context rife with career uncertainty. By drawing on life histories of ten young graduates and ten final-year students of the University of Dar es Salaam in Tanzania, I explore different ways through which young people meaningfully engage with their uncertain future(s).[1] Theoretical inspirations for this paper come from Emirbayer and Mische's (1998) theorisation of human agency, which pays attention to temporal orientations in the everyday practices of young graduates. This conception of human agency allows us to analyse young graduates as agents who actively and creatively strive for desired social adulthood even in the midst of uncertainties. Two immediate questions are central to this chapter.

---

1 | Although social actors are often concerned with the future in many regards, this concern has not until recently received due attention in social sciences such as Sociology and Anthropology (see Mische 2009).

First, what does it mean for a young individual to graduate in a context rife with career uncertainty? Second, how do young graduates meaningfully and actively engage with career uncertainties before and after graduating?

## Contextual issues: Situating graduates' career expectations

Tanzania envisages producing 80,000 graduates per year as articulated in one of the targets of the Tanzania Development Vision 2025 (URT 2005).[2] The government's ambition is increasing in scale, and recently the minister for Education and Vocational Training stated that the country aims to reach the target of annually enrolling 300,000 students at its universities by 2025. Interestingly, the Tanzania Development Vision 2025 grounds the importance of increasing the population of the country's graduates in the understanding that ›modernity‹ cannot be reached without a critical mass of diverse and well-educated people at the level of higher education. Therefore the vision underlines that,

Tanzania envisages to be a nation whose people are ingrained with a developmental mindset and competitive spirit. These attributes are driven by education and knowledge and are critical in enabling the nation to effectively utilize knowledge in mobilizing domestic resources for assuring the provision of people's basic needs and for attaining competitiveness in the regional and global economy. (URT 2005: 4)

To achieve that end, the vision stresses the necessity of producing »the quantity and quality of educated people sufficiently equipped with the requisite knowledge to solve the society's problems, meet the challenges of development and attain competitiveness at regional and global levels« (ibid.: 4).

---

**2** | The Tanzania Development Vision 2025 is one of the policy frameworks guiding the country towards attaining »development«. It was developed with an understanding that »a vision for development is an articulation of a desirable future condition or situation which a nation envisages to attain and the plausible course of action to be taken for its achievement [...]. It is a vehicle of hope and an inspiration for motivating the people to search and work harder for the betterment of their livelihood and for posterity« (URT 2005).

It cannot come as a surprise, then, that there is a burgeoning number of higher-learning institutions in a country which now already contains about 77 universities (Tanzania Commission for Universities 2015). Similarly relevant policy articulations are evident in the National Employment Policy of 2008, whose specific objectives include (but are not limited to) enhancing skills and competencies of the labour force; promoting the goal of decent and productive employment as a national priority; and promoting access to employment opportunities and resources for so-called vulnerable and marginalised groups such as youth, women and people with disabilities (URT 2008).

However commendable these initiatives are, Tanzania is also increasingly witnessing massive unemployment and/or underemployment among graduates. The situation is unsatisfactory, especially when graduate unemployment is juxtaposed with the popular national and societal narrative that ›education is key to better life‹ (*elimu ni ufunguo wa maisha*). Put differently, both national policy articulations and societal discourses frame education as a panacea to individual, societal and national development. At the individual level this means that graduates are expected to secure better jobs and experience high standards of living. More specifically, graduates ought to be in a position to demonstrate to their families and communities the benefits of being educated by being able to support family members and joining the club of consumerism, amongst other ways of displaying ›the better life‹. As such, it is important to understand how young graduates strive to meet the afore-mentioned societal expectations in their efforts to attain desired adulthood[3] whilst struggling with career uncertainties.[4]

## Young graduate unemployment in Tanzania

Graduate unemployment and/or underemployment is a reality in Tanzania, just like it is in other African countries (Mkude et al. 2003; Mihyo 2014). Presently, with over 70 public and private universities and

---

[3] | For a nuanced analysis on how young people in Africa struggle for a desired sense of being and becoming, see Christiansen, Utas and Vigh (2006); and Honwana and De Boeck (2005).

[4] | On how people deal with uncertainties in African, see Haram and Yamba (2009).

university colleges in Tanzania, it is estimated that 70,000 graduates enter the labour market each year but that only 4,000 (5.7 per cent) find formal employment (Massawe 2014).

Several factors including, amongst others, economic liberalisation, population growth and the growing education sector are believed to contribute to the situation of growing unemployment among graduates. Mkude, Cooksey and Levey (2003) underline that in the context of economic liberalisation, the privatisation of parastatal corporations and growth of the private economy have led to a freeze in government recruitment and downsizing, which have resulted in graduate unemployment in Tanzania (see also Mukyanuzi 2003).

Other studies have blamed the education policies and system(s) for fuelling graduate unemployment by not responding to the requirements of the labour market. For instance, Simon (2013) emphatically appeals to the need for learning institutions to prepare students in a manner that allows them to fit in the labour market. Likewise, Massawe (2014) argues that the education offered to youth in Tanzania is not particularly relevant to the needs of the Tanzanian labour market. For him most of the graduates are not only ill-prepared to enter the labour market but, indeed, unemployable. A study by the Inter-University Council of East Africa (IUCEA) supports this view in that it recently established that most graduates in the region were not fully prepared for the job market. In wider comparison, Kenya, Rwanda and Burundi were better off than Uganda or Tanzania (see IUCEA 2014).

Governments are concerned about youth unemployment not only because it is one of the biggest obstacles to economic growth but also due to the potential risk of triggering social upheaval (see URT 2008; IUCEA 2014). This is in line with what Honwana and De Boeck (2005) have underlined when they claim that »in Africa, young people not only constitute the majority of the population but they are also at the centre of societal interactions and transformation.« Nonetheless, the lived experience of young graduates in terms of how they engage with the uncertainty of securing employment remains unclear. This study was designed to analyse the lived experiences of young graduates from a department of the University of Dar es Salaam in Tanzania and aims to shed light on this gap in our knowledge.

## Conceptual framework

Engaging with questions about career expectations and the future requires us to pay attention to how individual actors deal with the future in meaningful and creative ways. This calls for a refined theorisation of agency that is capable of teasing out all interrelated dimensions of human agency. According to Emirbayer and Mische (1998), human agency is characterised by forms of actions oriented towards three temporal orientations: the habitual (oriented towards the past), the projective (towards the future) and the judgmental (towards the present). Emirbayer and Mische (ibid.) define human agency as:

the temporally constructed engagement by actors of different structural environments which entail temporal-relational contexts of action which through the interplay of habit, imagination and judgment, both reproduces and transforms those structures in interactive response to problems posed by changing historical situations.

No single action is entirely oriented towards the past, future or the present; rather, certain forms of actions are more oriented towards the past, the future or the present. Put differently, certain actions are more habitual while others demand more imagination or judgment. Thus, in every social action there is interplay between the three dimensions of agency, although the degree of dominance varies – meaning that one dimension can be more prominent in certain situations compared to other dimensions. For instance, graduating as a critical moment, or what Johnson-Hanks (2002) calls a »vital conjuncture«, triggers certain actions on the part of the young graduate, but these actions are more likely to be oriented towards the future. However, this does not mean that the young graduate in question does not care about situating her or his actions within the present while simultaneously drawing on one's own past experiences or those of others.

The above conception of agency, I argue, allows us to make sense of how and why young graduates, as social actors, actively engage with their uncertain futures before and after graduation. Indeed, this way of approaching young graduates demands discovering both proactive and reactive responses to career uncertainties in the lived experiences of the graduates. Here young graduates are not reduced to mere victims of graduate unemployment but, instead, are social actors who understand their situations and situate themselves accordingly in the course of pursuing their careers. More importantly, the nuances in the diverse and complex lived experiences of young graduates can be adequately explained.

## Career Aspirations Versus Lived Experiences

Graduates have a clear sense of what they want to be in the future. This sense of ›becoming‹ is developed along with societal expectations, lived or shared experiences and personal interests (see also Christiansen, Utas and Vigh 2006). From the experiences of my informants, choosing a career is a social rather than individual phenomenon. It can take different courses: while it is a highly contested process for some, it is quite smooth and pragmatic for others. In both cases, however, the actors in question are actively engaging with their futures. What is important to note though is that career choices are situated and dependent on specific contexts, which is why different informants grappled with different circumstances when deciding on what constituted their desired career(s).

To aspire to a career involves projecting certain expectations into the respective career. The crucial question in this chapter is how graduates in Tanzania (re)assess their career expectations at the end of their studies or after graduating. This calls for interrogating expectations against lived experiences. To this end, I have generated narratives from the discussion I conducted with a segment of students in their final year, and those who had recently graduated from the Department of Sociology at the University of Dar es Salaam.

## Motives for Pursuing a Particular Career

There are multiple factors that necessitate young graduates to struggle for a particular career. For many graduates involved in this study having a job or the means to earn income is not an end in itself but, rather, allows an individual to command access to resources that satisfy basic needs. For many others it also means the ability to support families, relatives and friends, and hence ensures a greater degree of social networks or social capital (Bourdieu 1990). Most of my informants, and in particular those who had graduated, reported that they had been providing some support to their family members in terms of for example cash, clothing and school fees. Indeed, some are already parents and therefore responsible for their own immediate families in addition to members of their extended family. It is important to note at this juncture that despite on-going social changes which increasingly favour the nuclear family, the traditional extended family structure still persists, at least in the practices of everyday life. Family members may not necessarily live together in the same compound, yet a strong sense of family ties is maintained through helping one another in times of need, as mentioned above.

Closely linked to this is the strong sense of belonging to a respectable social category or being able to acquire desired social identities and images – what Bourdieu (1990) refers to as symbolic capital. The latter pre-occupies the minds and efforts of the young graduates when they select a career to pursue, and even more so after they graduate. Consistent with the famous imaginary in Tanzania (i.e., ›education is key to better life‹), desired images of belonging to a ›better-off‹ social category entails attributes such as owning fashionable, sophisticated and expensive gadgets, or what Fuglesang (1994) refers to as »items of modernity«. Other attributes include ownership of car(s) and houses that are often posh in nature, and being able to afford the education of one's children at so-called ›international‹ and often expensive schools.

Most important here is the ability to display consumerism by spending money in what Ritzer (2008) has termed the »cathedrals of consumption«, including shopping malls and other popular leisure spaces. According to him, cathedrals of consumption are places of hyper-consumption that are built on a massive scale which enchants many consumers. These social spaces are designed in anticipation that consumers will gradually develop a passion for acquiring goods and services after experiencing what Ritzer (ibid.) has called a »spectacle«, which refers to varied forms of attention-grabbing strategies geared towards attracting consumers. Accordingly, the spectacle has a tendency to lead people to consume far more than necessary. As rightly pointed out by Ritzer (2005), cathedrals of consumption have been »aggressively exported to the rest of the world«, including to Tanzania. Indeed, there is a significant mushrooming of home-grown cathedrals of consumption in most of the cities and towns in Tanzania today.

One of the key findings of the majority of discussions and interviews with young graduates is that most of the graduates aspire to have well-paying jobs and/or enterprises which would provide them with the ability to meet a combination of ends, as discussed above. Given the uncertainties that young graduates are confronted with in real life, the immediate question is how they deal with such problematic experiences, and I now turn my attention to this matter.

## Methods

This chapter draws on my one-year-long qualitative study of ten young graduates and ten final-year undergraduate students from the Department of Sociology at the University of Dar es Salaam in Tanzania. In his reflection on the role of sociology in Africa a decade ago, Chachage (2004) observed that doing sociology was »among the lucrative activities« in Tanzania (and Africa in general) due to the demand for sociologists in development programmes. Although this is still the case in today's Tanzania and throughout Africa, the labour market is increasingly flooded with sociologists. Thus, graduates and final-year undergraduate students from the Department of Sociology provided relevant cases for the understanding of what it means to graduate in a context of career uncertainties. The study was conducted between January and December 2014.

Through a round of interviews and discussions with graduates, the study generated life histories and narratives about career choices and expectations as well as the lived experiences of informants. Four rounds of encounters with informants were undertaken along with two focus group discussions (FGDs), one of which was conducted with final-year students and the other with graduates. Because most of the informants were either my own final-year students or former students of mine, reflexivity was critical at every step of the research process so as to overcome the threat that my position could influence the results. Therefore, I involved a research assistant to conduct selected interviews especially with final-year students, and to assist in facilitating FGDs with the students. Another strategy I adopted in an attempt to grasp informants' emic perspectives was to situate every piece of data within the context of the respective informant, especially during data interpretation. The study adopted constant comparative analysis as its analytical strategy and was informed by Grounded Theory. This has allowed me to develop a typology of proactive and reactive engagements of young graduates in the context of uncertain futures. In addition to a small number of quotations from interviews, a description and synthesis of graduates' lived experiences is provided along with selected portraits and vignettes. For the sake of anonymity, the names used in the portraits are not my informants' real names.

## Negotiating the Future: Proactive and Reactive Response(s) to Career Uncertainty

Diverse proactive and reactive engagements with career uncertainty characterise the lived experiences of many young graduates in Tanzania. These include, but are not limited to, attracting potential employers through volunteering and/or internships; taking up temporary jobs within and beyond one's field of expertise; and a temporary or permanent change of career, that is, taking up employment opportunities in other fields. In addition, running some form of business, temporarily returning to one's home, and pursuing postgraduate studies are also equally important responses to career uncertainty. The matrix below summarises the main findings of the study.

Analytically, Emirbayer and Mische (1998) suggest that graduates' concern with their future (projectivity) is triggered by problematic situations and the challenges of social life posed by career uncertainty. As agents, young graduates engage in the »hypothesization of experience«, or what Herbert Mead refers to as »distance experience«. This invokes activities that fall into the category of imagination. In practical terms, actors in such situations – the formation of projects (using Alfred Schutz's notion of project) – attempt to *reconfigure* or transform (at least in a temporal sense) the pre-established patterns. Here, Emirbayer and Mische (1998) assert:

Immersed in a temporal flow, they [the *actors*] move beyond themselves into the future and construct changing images of where they think they are going, where they want to go, and how they can get there from where they are at present. Such *images* […] entail proposed interventions at diverse and intersecting levels of social life. […] *Projectivity* is thus located in a critical *mediating juncture* between the iterational (past) and practical-evaluative (present) aspects of agency. (Emphasis added; see also Sambaiga 2013: 47; Johnson-Hanks 2002.)

Indeed, the lived experiences presented below reflect processes which, following Emirbayer and Mische (1998), are profoundly critical for projectivity: anticipatory identification, narrative construction, symbolic recomposition, hypothetical resolution and symbolic experimental enactment.[5]

*Proactive and reactive responses of young graduates in relation to career uncertainties*

| Proactive/reactive Responses | Examples |
|---|---|
| Attracting potential employers | Volunteering and/or internship: while some secure employment within the organisations where they volunteered or did their internships, others use the experience and skills gained to secure jobs in other organisations |
| Taking up temporary jobs within and beyond one's field of expertise | Research assistant, customer service provider, credit officer, bank teller, secondary-school teacher, etc – sometimes transforming these into permanent jobs |
| Temporary or permanent change of career | Taking up employment opportunities in other fields – often not by choice but necessity |

---

**5 | I:** *Anticipatory identification* points to the important fact that horizons of alternative possibilities are often presented to the actor in a vague and uncertain way. It also means that the actor will have to engage with his or her stock of knowledge (in the words of Alfred Schütz) in a retrospective manner;
II: *Narrative construction*: the construction of narratives simply provides the actor with a vehicle to imagine or locate future possibilities, yet narratives are not themselves projects;
III: *Symbolic recomposition*: ways in which actors playfully insert themselves into a variety of possible courses of action and snatch alternative opportunities, which in turn expand their flexible response (as actors) to a given field of action; this is what Emirbayer and Mische (1998) and Certeau (1984) refer to as tactic – as well as its inherent capacity to impose itself in the spaces of others;
IV: *Hypothetical (or imaginary) resolution* entails the task of identifying potentially appropriate resolutions for multiple and often contradicting concerns, i.e. moral, cultural, economic, practical and emotional demands;
V: *Experimental enactment* sits at the margin (or borderline) between imagination and action, that is, between the future and the present. Once scenarios have been examined and solutions proposed, these hypothetical resolutions may be put to the test (by the actors) in tentative or exploratory social interactions.

| Running some kind of business(es) | Initiatives under this category are popularly referred to as *ujasiriamali* (entrepreneurships) or *kujiajili* (self-employment). This has also been institutionalised as *the informal sector* |
|---|---|
| Pursuing postgraduate studies | If they can afford it, some graduates resort to postgraduate studies |
| Taking up a political career | Increasingly, graduates are entering into politics at different levels |

It is tempting to assume that there is a rigid limit between the proactive and reactive engagements if we attempt to confine the practices into a dichotomy of those enacted before and after graduation. However, lived experiences of young graduates (presented below) suggest that both proactive and reactive responses are transcendental in nature. While some proactive engagements are adopted prior to graduating, others are enacted after graduation and/or when one is already employed. In the same vein, what constitutes a reactive response (or several responses) for one graduate may be a proactive response for another. There are also cases where an initially proactive response turns into a reactive response to cope with career uncertainty. As such, the social practise, or ›projects‹, enacted by young graduates in the course of dealing with career uncertainties are as fluid in nature as is the transition between graduation and (un)employment. How and when an individual graduate takes up one or a combination of the aforementioned response(s) to career uncertainty is a subject to which I now turn.

First, attracting potential employers is an increasingly popular approach among graduates and university students. It involves an assessment on the part of the actors to identify organisations in which they see potential for employment or through which they could gain specific experiences or skills. Informants repeatedly mentioned using two major proactive approaches here to entice potential employers: securing an internship position in the organisation in question, or working as a volunteer. The two approaches are considered to be more suitable for graduates without any previous work experience because they are able to gain the specific experiences and skills required by many employers.

My informants in their final year of studies had either volunteered or completed an internship in one or more organisations at one point in time during their long vacations. Others had applied for placement as volunteers or become interns upon finishing their studies. Similarly, graduates who were already employed or searching for employment confirmed that they had worked as volunteers and/or interns during the time they had been searching for employment. While there are those who managed to secure employment within the organisations where they volunteered or did their internships (see Rasheeda's portrait below), many others said that the experience and skills they had gained enabled them to secure jobs in other organisations.

However, to be an intern or volunteer is not unproblematic, especially in regard to subsistence, since many organisations do not pay salaries to graduates or students. This means that although some graduates wish to volunteer or take up internship positions, they are unable to do this due to financial constraints. Others reported to have been forced to stop volunteering because they could no longer afford either the costs of transport to and from the organisation's location or their own subsistence.

### Rasheeda Abdul tells her internship story

Rasheeda graduated from the Department of Sociology and Anthropology of the University of Dar es Salaam in 2011. She is one of those graduates who converted her internship into employment. She says that she secured an internship position in an organisation working on HIV/AIDS prevention in the Kagera Region known as International Care, Adherence and Prevention of HIV and AIDS (ICAP).

Rasheeda completed her practical training (PT) in this organisation in the second year of her studies. The familiarity that was created during the PT became a conduit through which she was accepted as an intern. The driving force behind her search for an internship largely arose from the difficulty of acquiring employment after graduation and the uncertainty of doing so in the near future. Rasheeda confirms that she opted for internship because she was worried about going through the same difficult experiences faced by her friends and relatives who had graduated in recent years. She has seen many graduates remain jobless and unemployed for a number of years after graduation. She learnt from others' experiences and heeded the advice of friends

> and close relatives, and therefore searched for an internship, which she soon acquired in February 2012. Rasheeda worked as an intern for about a year before ICAP announced vacant positions in the Psychosocial Support Department; she applied and was able to secure a two-year employment contract. When I approached Rasheeda for interviews, she was still working with ICAP.
>
> Reflecting on the internship experience and dynamics, Rasheeda summed up that »internship is not ›a cup of tea‹ [...]. It is coupled with many challenges such as inadequate or no formal payment except for a few advantages you gain when there are outreach trips, workshops and training sessions, or sometimes friendly offerings from the employed staff.«
>
> Nonetheless, for Rasheeda internship was a means towards acquiring employment.

The lived experience of Rasheeda illuminates how young graduates relate to time and space in their search for employment opportunities. Here the future presents itself in form of aspirations of becoming employed and/or avoiding unemployment. Building on the experiences of other graduates (many of whom are unemployed), Rasheeda proactively engages with her future by searching for an internship. Above all, she puts up with the challenges of working as an intern in the hope that the skills and experiences she gains will function as resources in her future endeavour to search for employment. Although this case is representative of the experiences of many graduates who succeed in securing employment in their desired professions, there are many others who are forced to take up employment opportunities not related to their fields of expertise. This is a practice to which I now turn.

Taking up temporary jobs within and beyond one's field of expertise is another responsive engagement used by young graduates in dealing with career uncertainty. Under pressure from a wide range of their own needs and societal expectations, some young sociology graduates find it necessary to accept temporary jobs both within and outside their field of expertise. This requires them to re-assess the future by paying attention to the present moment in the sense that young graduates ought to deal with their present situations in the course of searching for their desired future careers. This leads them for instance to work as research assistants on a short-term basis, to teach subjects other than sociology in secondary schools, and to work as bank tellers. These are often considered as coping strategies in the course of searching for desired jobs that fit well with individual graduates' aspired careers. It is important to note that, in the experiences of such graduates, the future is never rigid but fluid; in other words, graduates can change or shift their career aspirations after having had a particular experience. Jobs that were initially meant to be temporary can end up being long-term or even permanent. For example, there are many young sociology graduates who work as freelance research assistants for up to four or more years after graduation. Some have developed wider networks for conducting research, which provide them with higher earnings than peers who are formally employed. The following portrait of Baraka Charles exemplifies young graduates' experiences with temporary jobs.

### Baraka Charles's experiences with temporary jobs

Baraka Charles graduated in 2013 from the Department of Sociology and Anthropology at the University of Dar es Salaam in Tanzania. He currently works as a teacher at Mapambano Tuition Centre in Dar es Salaam – a job that he considers to be temporary while he continues to look for a job to which he aspires. Baraka Charles started working as a part-time teacher at Mapambano Tuition even before graduating because he did not have full sponsorship. He was only sponsored for 20 per cent by the Higher Education Students Loans Board (HESLB), which means that he was obliged to contribute 80 per cent of the 1.3 million Tanzania shillings due in tuition fees himself. Given the poverty of his parents, Baraka was forced to pay this sum from the meals and accommodation allowances he received from the sponsoring organisation. Baraka had so little cash left over that he was unable to fulfil his subsistence needs besides purchasing academic requisites such as stationery and the like. Therefore Baraka was forced to look for temporary or part-time jobs. He managed to secure a part-time teaching post at Mapambano Tuition Centre, where he started teaching students who had registered for re-sitting their ordinary or advanced secondary education. Interestingly, after his graduation Baraka started to apply for every opportunity that came his way which required a candidate of his calibre; nevertheless he had not yet secured formal employment in line with his career expectations. Nonetheless, Baraka was earning a living through teaching at the Tuition Centre as well as other centres that periodically hired him. Showing that this experience is not unique to him, Baraka recounted that »this is not peculiar to me. I know of many teachers here at Mapambano Tuition Centre, including those who own the Centre, who have passed along a similar trajectory, and we are receiving applications from many graduates asking for the same opportunities.«

The attraction of getting employed, alongside the need to meet various expectations as well as the demands of everyday life, have led graduates to challenge their previous career choices. Rather than choosing between careers, the context of unemployment necessitates pragmatic action on the part of the graduate in order to respond to the »demands and contingencies of the present« (Emirbayer and Mische 1998). This is manifested in the decision to change one's career. For instance, sociology graduates increasingly find work as bank tellers, credit officers, customer service providers in telecommunication companies, and secondary-school teachers not by choice but by necessity. Apaiha Ngowi's experience in changing careers further illustrates how young graduates shift between careers in order to cope with unemployment.

### Apaiha Ngowi's shift in career aspirations

When she graduated from the University of Dar Es Salaam in 2012, Apaiha's wanted to work as a counsellor because she had specialised in Medical Sociology and completed a number of courses on guidance, counselling and social psychology. Her prospects for the future were not to work as a private counsellor (because this is not a recognised profession in Tanzania) but, instead, to work at one of the big hospitals in the country.

> Immediately after her graduation and in line with her career aspirations, Apaiha applied for a post as a counsellor at three or more public hospitals and four private hospitals. After waiting anxiously to be called to either an interview or job placement in vain, Apaiha decided to go and talk to the respective authorities about her applications. Unfortunately, none of the hospitals considered her application.
> Under pressure from concrete livelihood demands in her everyday life, Apaiha decided to apply for any job that came her way. »Luckily,« according to her, she secured a customer care job with Vodacom Network Provider at Mlimani City in Dar es Salaam. She reported that she had held that position for eighteen months but was later placed in the new department of procurement and logistics. Apaiha confirms that she still has a deep desire to work as a counsellor but that reality on the ground has yet to offer her the opportunity. According to Apaiha, the everyday needs and expectations from parents and siblings forced her to opt for another means for subsistence. Rethinking her previous career aspirations, Apaiha now considers pursuing a different specialisation in her Master's degree that could fit better with the available job opportunities. Hence, she is thinking of studying for a Master's degree in Business Administration (MBA) with a focus on procurement.

Similarly, running a form of business is increasingly considered and/or used by young graduates as both proactive and reactive engagement with career uncertainty. Initiatives under this category are popularly termed *ujasiriamali* (entrepreneurships) or *kujiajili* (self-employment) and institutionalised as part of the informal sector. Some graduates had started business projects when they were still pursuing their university studies. Jasmine Zubery (portrait below) is a case in point. Two other final-year students I interviewed were running businesses which sold utilities to their fellow students, including pants, handbags and mobile phones. Opening a hair-dressing saloon is another type of business project that is frequently undertaken. Interestingly, start-up capital was generated from various sources, including what is commonly known as *boom* – funds provided to students as a loan by the government through Institution

Students Loan Board. The *boom* is meant to cover students' subsistence costs but it can easily be manipulated by, for example, transforming it into capital for business projects.[6]

Graduates have also generated start-up capital through short-term employment. Others secure loans from banks or micro-credit associations. While some run business projects and continue to be employed, others – especially those who become successful in their business – may quit employment or feel disenchanted in seeking employment (if they are not yet employed). For instance, one of my female informants, who had graduated with her first degree five years earlier, decided to start an informal micro-credit scheme. The scheme entails lending money at an often higher interest rate to people whom she either knows or are recommended by people she knows. During the four rounds of interviews I conducted with her, she reiterated the fact that she earns enough money and therefore cannot imagine being employed at the moment. Although she was about to complete her Master's degree in sociology, she categorically pointed out that she regrets doing postgraduate studies because she does not plan to seek employment.

However, there are many others who would wish to start business projects yet cannot generate start-up capital. Another female graduate, who is married with two children, had worked with three different organisations since her graduation ten years earlier. Her last contract ended in 2011 and since then she has been applying for jobs in vain, with the exception of temporary opportunities as a research assistant. Such assistantships are not often available for her, and hence she has considered starting her own business. Inasmuch as this is something that she is ready to do, the challenge has consisted in discovering how to get the necessary start-up capital.

---

**6** | The *boom* has also been used to fund remittances, to supplement tuition fees for those whose loans do not cover 100 per cent of their tuition fees, and to purchase items of modernity such as mobile phones, television sets and computers.

### Jasmine Zubery: entrepreneurship as a means of dealing with graduate unemployment

When this study was conducted Jasmine Zubery was a third-year student in the Department of Sociology and Anthropology at the University of Dar es Salaam, and she was had been running a small business ever since her second year at university. Jasmine's case is representative of many students who did the same activities during their period of studies as a coping strategy in regard to the unfolding future. Her interest in starting a business alongside her studies originates in the experience she had with a few of her friends as well as her own two brothers, all of which spent more than three years without securing any formal employment despite completing their university studies. They were living from simple business activities and part-time jobs. Thus, for Jasmine starting a business was also inspired by the emerging business ventures that have come to involve many youngsters and, especially, undergraduates in what has come to be commonly known as ›business networking‹. According to her this business is only good and profitable if you can persuade more customers and businesspeople to join your line. The more businesspeople that you recruit under your name and under their names, the more points you gain; and these points translate into money. This is what ›networking‹ means here.

According to her, the business consists in buying and selling the company's products (called The Forever Living Products), which include body sprays, perfume and herbal products such as juice, shampoo, soap and detergents. She explains: »While we do this business we gain twice. In my case, first I buy products at lower prices and sell them at slightly higher prices; but, second, I also get a monthly bonus depending on the number of people I have pulled into this business.«

Jasmine got her start-up capital by generating modest funds from the *boom* and a little pocket money she received from her parents. Jasmine is convinced that she will not be under too much pressure in looking for formal employment from either the government or private companies since she runs her own small entrepreneurial business.

2 Negotiating the Future    47

Pursuing postgraduate studies is another means used by graduates to engage with their uncertain futures in regard to employment.w Conscious of the stiff competition on the labour market, some graduates consider postgraduate studies as a means to command a competitive advantage when it comes to seeking employment. Although few students like David Joseph (see portrait below) decide to pursue a postgraduate degree in sociology, many of the sociology graduates opt for programmes that seem to be more promising in terms of securing employment upon graduation (that is, they re-assess their aspirations). However, many find it difficult to afford the costs associated with pursuing postgraduate studies.

Joseph (see portrait below) decide to pursue a postgraduate degree in sociology, many of the sociology graduates opt for programmes that seem to be more promising in terms of securing employment upon graduation (that is, they re-assess their aspirations). However, many find it difficult to afford the costs associated with pursuing postgraduate studies.

### David Joseph: pursuing postgraduate studies as a strategy of coping with graduate unemployment

David Joseph is a postgraduate student doing a Master's degree in Sociology at the University of Dar es Salaam, whose motives for pursuing such a degree arose from his uncertain future prospects in terms of employability. David graduated in 2013 and started his Master's in Sociology in the same year. He recounts that he decided on postgraduate studies after looking at the employment situation and the employability of graduates in Tanzania and considering that a large number of young graduates from both public and private universities flock onto the labour market and that the annually announced vacancies available are limited. Starting his postgraduate studies was a chance for him to increase his credit and advantages on the labour market, the continuation of support from his parents and siblings (just like during the time when he had been an undergraduate), and it served as a transition period prior to getting employment. In fact, David continues to apply for jobs and attend interviews when short-listed. He believes that if he secures a ›good‹ job (meaning a well-paying job), he would look into the possibility of

> doing both his studies as well as the job; but should this not be possible, then he would choose the job and postpone his studies. Representative of a large proportion of young graduates, David says that this particular way of coping with graduate unemployment is adopted by many – and sometimes even much earlier, during undergraduate studies. Students who ›sense‹ the possibility that their families can support their postgraduate studies, start to persuade their parents and close relatives (sisters, brothers and uncles) to support them in pursuing further studies soon after they graduate. Like this, David still enjoys financial support from his parents while envisaging having a better job after the completion of his Master's degree.

Finally, pursuing a political career is increasingly becoming an option for young graduates in Tanzania. This is mainly due to the fact that high-level political positions such as being a Member of Parliament or a minister for the government, as well as top leadership posts within political parties, constitute lucrative careers in Tanzania today. Similarly, lower-level political posts such as Ward Councillors, who have the prospect of being Chairs of the District Council or municipal mayors, have also attracted young graduates' interest. Although only two of my informants had pursued a political career, there were several aspirants who considered pursuing a political career in the near future. Three of my informants reported that they had already joined an opposition political party with a view to establishing opportunities to obtain a political post.

To contextualise the interest in political careers, it is important to note that young graduates are very much aware of other graduates in sociology and other disciplines whose lives have improved considerably upon becoming a mayor or Member of Parliament – not to mention those who have become government ministers. Tumson Mwakipesile's case sheds light on this for us.

### Tumson Mwakipesile: taking up a political career

Tumson is a 2009 male graduate in sociology from the University of Dar Es Salaam, whose political career started when he was a first-year student in 2006. Tumson successfully became

> college representative in the Dar es Salaam University Students' Organisation (DARUSO) and was selected as Minister for Public Affairs in the same students' governing body. After his graduation Tumson did not secure a job but instead decided to work as a part-time teacher at various private schools before deciding to start a political career as a local Councillor for the Sisitila Ward in Mbeya City. He gained that position and was still working in that capacity at the time of the present study. His reflections on his decision to take up a political career indicate the struggle that Tumson and his peers go through in their efforts to deal with employment uncertainty. Tumson feels that he probably would not have secured employment if he had not decided to begin a political career. Tumson's feelings are anchored in his reference to the experiences of many of his fellow graduates, who continue to work part-time and run businesses in different places. When Tumson projects the future, he considers his political career to be promising, and he expects to achieve even more in the future, planning soon to become a Member of Parliament in one of the constituencies of Mbeya. For him politics can be an alternative path for unemployed graduates. Although Tumson confirms that his current political position is not financially lucrative, he commands much respect in the community and is able to meet his daily basic needs.

## Conclusion

In this chapter I have tackled the two major questions of what it means for a young person to graduate in a context rife with career uncertainties; and how young graduates meaningfully engage with their uncertain future(s) before and after graduating. This study clearly finds that the future in the lived experiences of young graduates is inscribed in hopes, expectations, desires, aspirations, optimism and/or pessimism. Young graduates in Tanzania are forced to (re)assess their desired career(s) against their lived experiences before and after graduation. This also means struggling to harmonise diverse individual and societal expectations and aspirations with concrete realities and lived experiences. Whereas for many young graduates graduating means facing an uncertain future, for others this event means embracing long-awaited opportunities. The latter group include (amongst others) those graduates who were already employed before joining the university.

Diverse proactive and reactive engagements with career uncertainty characterise the lived experiences of many young graduates in Tanzania. When deciding on which options and actions to take, young graduates are not only concerned with their present situation but also proactively deal with their futures. Young graduates resort to a wide range of responses, which include attracting potential employers by volunteering and/or starting an internship; taking up temporary jobs within and beyond one's field of expertise; and a temporary or permanent change of career, that is, taking up employment opportunities in other fields. Additional and equally important responses to career uncertainty are for graduates to run some kind of business(es), to temporarily return to one's home, and to pursue postgraduate studies. These responses are variously adopted either in sequence or simultaneously, depending on the situation or circumstances that individual graduates face in their everyday lives. Analytically, efforts to examine what it means for young graduate to graduate in a context like that of contemporary Tanzania, which is rife with career uncertainties, offer an important window for understanding how social actors engage with their future(s).

The findings of this study confirm the fact that often there is a mismatch between imagined futures (aspirations, expectations, hopes, desires and visions) and anticipated outcomes (Mische 2009). Importantly, however, these findings corroborate some sociological theorising on the future, specifically that »beliefs and expectations of the future in part determine what happens in the present by contributing to how people think, feel, and behave« (Zimbardo and Boyd 2008: 137). This allows us to explain the motives behind young graduates' engagement in the various proactive and/or reactive responses to career uncertainty that have been discussed in this contribution. Thus, as social actors, young graduates respond to problematic situations or uncertainties in their everyday life. Crucially however, these graduates deploy their forces and capabilities as agents in order to shape and open up future possibilities.

## Bibliography

Al-Samarrai, Samer, Paul Bennell. 2007. »Where Has All the Education Gone in Sub-Saharan Africa? Employment and Other Outcomes among Secondary School and University Leavers.« *The Journal of Development Studies* 43(7): 1270–1300.

Bourdieu, Pierre. 1990. *The Logic of Practice*. Stanford: Stanford University Press.

Certeau, Michel de. 1984. *The Practice of Everyday Life*. Berkeley: University of California.

Chachage, Seithy Loth. 2004. »Sociology and the Future: Resistance, Reconstruction and Democracy.« *Society in Transition* 35(1): 42–60.

Christiansen, Catrine, Mats Utas, Henrik E. Vigh. 2006. *Navigating Youth, Generating Adulthood: Social Becoming in an African Context*. Uppsala: Nordic Africa Institute.

Emirbayer, Mustafa, Ann Mische. 1998. »What Is Agency?« *American Journal of Sociology* 103(4): 962–1023.

Fuglesang, Minou. 1994. »Veils and Videos: Female Youth Culture on the Kenyan Coast.« PhD dissertation, Stockholm University.

Haram, Liv, C. Bawa Yamba. 2009. *Dealing with Uncertainty in Contemporary African Lives*. Uppsala: Nordic African Institute.

Honwana, Alcinda, Filip De Boeck. 2005. *Makers & Breakers: Children and Youth in Postcolonial Africa*. Oxford: James Currey.

IEUCEA. 2014. »Report from a Study Establishing the Status of Higher Education Qualifications Systems and Their Contributions to Human Resources Development in East Africa.«

Johnson-Hanks, Jennifer. 2002. »On the Limits of Life Stages in Ethnography: Toward a Theory of Vital Conjunctures.« *American Anthropologist* 104(3): 865–880.

Massawe, Deogratius. 2014. »Urban Youth Unemployment in Tanzania: Analysis of Causes and Policy Responses.« In *Employment Policies and Unemployment in Eastern and Southern Africa*, edited by Organisation for Social Science Research in Eastern and Southern Africa.

Mead, George Herbert. 1932. *The Philosophy of the Present*. Chicago: University of Chicago Press.

Mische, Ann. 2009. »Projects and Possibilities: Researching Futures in Action.« *Sociological Forum* 24(3): 694–704.

Mkude, Daniel, Brian Cooksey, Lisbeth Levey. 2003. *Higher Education in Tanzania: A Case Study*. Oxford: James Currey.

Mukyanuzi, Faustin. 2003. *Where Has All the Eduction Gone in Tanzania? Employment Outcomes Among Seconday School and University Leavers*. Brighton: Institute of Development Studies at the University of Sussex.

Paschal B. Mihyo. 2014. *Employment Policies and Unemployment in Eastern and Southern Africa*. Addis Ababa: OSSREA Publications.

Ritzer, George. 2005. *Enchanting a Disenchanted World: Revolutionizing the Means of Consumption*. Thousand Oaks: Pine Forge Press.

—. 2008. *The McDonaldization of Society 5*. Thousand Oaks: Pine Forge Press.

Sambaiga, Richard Faustine. 2013. *Sexual Inter-Subjectivity and the Quest for Social Well-Being: An Ethnographic Inquiry of Adolescent Sexuality and Reproduction in Urban Southern Tanzania*. Basel: University of Basel.

Schütz, Alfred. 1962. Choosing among Projects of Action. In *Collected Papers: The Problem of Social Reality*. Volume 1, ed. M. Natanson. The Hague: Martinus Nijhoff, pp. 67–96.

Simon, Peter. 2013. *Nature Of Urban Youth Unemployment In Tanzania: Challenges And Consequences*. Dar es Salaam: Repoa.

Tanzania Commission for Universities. 2015. *Undergraduate Students Admission Guidebook for Higher Education Institutions in Tanzania*. Dar es Salaam: TCU.

United Republic of Tanzania. 2005. *Tanzania Development Vision 2025*. Dar es Salaam: MoF.

United Republic of Tanzania 2008. *National Employment Policy*. Dar es Salaam: Ministry of Labour Employment and Youth Development.

Zimbardo, Philip, John Boyd. 2008. *The Time Paradox: The New Psychology of Time That Will Change Your Life*. New York: Simon and Schuster.

# 3 Ça va aller

The Role of Hope in Burkinabe University Graduates' Navigation towards the Future

*Maike Birzle*

## INTRODUCTION:
## BEING A YOUNG GRADUATE IN BURKINA FASO

Malik is a young Burkinabe who graduated from the University of Ouagadougou in 2012. He holds a diploma in economics, yet he is still looking for employment. When I first met him in 2013 he was 33 years of age; this makes him the oldest graduate in my research sample of thirty freshly-graduated diploma-holders. He lives in a small compound in a neighbourhood called »Zone 1«, which is characterised by a high number of students attracted by modest houses with low rents close to their university, where he shares his cramped two-room apartment with two of his cousins who recently also started to study at the university. Like him, they are »Diaspo«, that is, their families migrated from Burkina Faso to Ivory Coast in search of work opportunities. For Malik being »Diaspo« means that the network of relatives who support him financially at irregular intervals is distant and not easy to access. The living room of his apartment is crammed with chairs along the walls, and there is little space for the television set and a table cluttered with exercise books and papers. Most of these are workbooks for the annual *concours*, which is a recruitment test for the civil service. Malik bases all of his hope on the slim chance of being amongst the small number of applicants recruited each year. He is aware that time is not on his side because the maximum age for participation is 37. Therefore, he invests all affordable means in training-books and preparation classes. When I met him in 2014 and 2015 he had not yet found a job. In 2016 he wrote to me explaining that he would prepare for the recruitment test in 2017 – still convinced that finally he would be lucky enough to be on the winning side. Despite numerous setbacks Malik holds on to his optimism, and whenever I met him he was always in good humour and confident about the future. Yet, he also spoke of sleepless nights full of fears about what the next day would bring. His thoughts circle around the fact that he is still dependent on his parents and brothers – and on the crop yield of their cocoa fields in Ivory Coast – in order to make a living, despite having spent so much time and money on his university studies. Malik meets his graduated peers nearly every day in the shade of the trees on the university campus to discuss exercise after exercise from the workbooks for the *concours*, hoping to increase his chances by training from early morning until late afternoon. Indeed, hope is an important topic not only in Malik's narrations and actions. In this chapter I ask what hope means for him and the other graduates to whom I have spoken in their orientation towards the future. In order to do this I draw upon participant observation and consecutive interviews with thirty young graduates, all of which were conducted between 2013 and 2015 in Ouagadougou and Bobo.

After they complete their studies, graduates are confronted with demands for financial support by their families as well as social pressure to get married and start their own family. However, instead of being able to follow what they had imagined to be a straightforward trajectory (employment followed by marriage and then children), they are forced to deal with detours and delays; instead of proceeding as they had imagined when they were still students, they approach their goals in ways which often seem to be indirect. Amongst my informants there is the notion that the future has to be accessed through certain entry points, which are imagined as gateways. Interviewees reflected on the future in a way that suggests that they imagine there to be a cleavage between the present and the future which prevents individuals from realising their plans either quickly or straightforwardly. In the following I elaborate upon how this cleavage is manifested. I will show how young Burkinabe graduates implement the idea of accessing the future by imagining their trajectories as a kinetic process, which gains dynamism through their active hope and thereby serves to create accessible gateways. These dynamics are also influenced by the obstacles they encounter when they try to implement their plans. The point of departure for this chapter is the observation that the majority of my informants present themselves as

»not yet having arrived« in the place they want to be in order to be satisfied with their situation. I will use the concept of ›social navigation‹ to trace the (narratively reflected) motion of graduates towards their future goals. Vigh (2009: 419) introduces this concept in order to facilitate a better understanding of practices in contexts of insecurity and uncertainty, in other words, of motion in a fluctuating framework. The concept is open for discontinuities in individual action, which is especially relevant in the case of Burkinabe graduates in regard to the adaption and transformation of their goals. Although they approach these goals in ways that they often perceive as being indirect, they thereby transform their environment into a terrain in which they are able to manoeuvre in order to attain them (Jackson 1998). In this way they navigate their social present while trying to influence their individual and collective futures by outlining ways that lead to their goals. This reveals that they are far from being trapped, despite the fact that direct routes towards their goals are often blocked. In order to carve out the conditions of their capacities to navigate, I will analyse how young graduates discursively reflect on their current situation and present activities, and the way in which they locate their pathways into the future.

University studies in Burkina Faso are seen as gate-openers to a better life by all of my informants. Most of them stated this fact as their personal motivation to study at university, and the conviction that university diplomas greatly facilitate entry into the Burkinabe job market is fundamental. They believe that holding a diploma leads to a greater number of entry points becoming available, that the salary will be higher and that more interesting posts will be available. The higher the diploma, the higher the salary, is a commonly held notion amongst my informants. Besides this factor, several mentioned that their initial motivation to study at university was to become able to support their parents financially, which is an aspect of the motivation for finding well-paid employment. Other aspects mentioned were the wish for a better understanding of things, for personal success and for the possibility to contribute to the country's development. It becomes clear that finding a job is a basic ambition when informants explain that they had been participating in the annual competition for posts in the civil service ever since they obtained their *baccalaureat* (high school diploma) but, because they had not yet succeeded, they were continuing their studies at university in order to find a job later on. About two-thirds of my sample had tried this strategy, but none of them became employed and left their studies. A graduate of economics explained that he dreamt of working for an international bank, but when he started university studies he also had in mind that after two years of studies he could, as he said, at least work as a teacher in the civil service. He nevertheless continued until he obtained his diploma. The *baccalaureat* alone is not enough to find employment in Burkina Faso today, my informants agree. Several graduates whom I interviewed explained that their motivation was also influenced by their parents, who had urged them to go to university. The motivation factors often intersect, as in the case of Cynthia:

MB: What made you start studying at university?
Cynthia: (laughing) I always told myself that it has to be interesting to have a diploma and knowledge in order to be primed to work in international enterprises; that is the reason why I wanted to study at university. And my parents also urged me and told me not to stop at only the high school diploma, because high-school diplomas are nothing anymore. (Cynthia, 28, accountant; Interview July 2013, my translation.)

When asked about their current situation about a year after their graduation, nearly all informants replied that they were still looking for employment. Exceptions were two young women who studied medicine, one of whom had entered the civil service and worked at a public hospital, and the other who is now a doctor at a private clinic. Unemployment in the case of university graduates in Burkina Faso does not equate to inactivity in terms of generating income but, instead, is used to explain that they have not yet found a job that is commensurable to their university diploma.

## *Ça va aller:* Narrations and Manifestations of Unpredictability

When faced with unpredictability that includes the delayed entry into the job market, the ever-present phrase to be encountered is »*ça va aller*« (it will work out alright), which is always intertwined with the notion that higher education must eventually and inevitably lead to benefits. »*Ça va aller*« is like a chorus and is voiced in nearly every interview when the speaker refers to the future and its unpredictability. Retelling this phrase seems like a narrative obligation, for example when a young graduate says:

»like every good citizen I tell myself *ça va aller*.« (Yacouba, 28, graduate of geology; Interview March 2014, my translation.) Yet, the interviews also make clear that there is more to this phrase than its talismanic invocation suggests. Analysing the passages where »*ça va aller*« is expressed, several patterns of usage emerge. The principal function of the phrase is narrative and practical in that it enables the speaker to shift from a negative point in the narration to a more positive projection upon which they can then further elaborate. This appears in two senses. First, this relates to a condition that is seen as normal or favourable, for example when saying that the political system is unfavourable while hoping that it will change or be ameliorated; or for example when one anticipates that having two children in the future would be a good condition. There is always a dynamic aspect to the phrase, thereby implying a comparative characteristic:

I appreciate my current situation compared to the one before, because it brings along autonomy and now I hope that it will work out much better in the future [*maintenant j'espère que ça va aller beaucoup mieux dans l'avenir*]. (Sandrine, 29, graduate in law studies; Interview February 2014, my translation.)

Second – and far more frequently – the phrase is used as a metaphor. Like this it serves to bridge a rift which is formed by the unpredictability of future events. The phrase becomes a place-holder in interviews, and I will interpret its intended meaning by analyzing the respective sequences. When used as a metaphor it always refers to an event that serves as a catalyst in transforming the now-condition, which is unfavourable for several reasons, into a favourable afterward-condition. For example:

I'm trying to find something, and often, after I receive responses like in the job interview this morning, I tell myself that little-by-little it will pay off, and that is reassuring. I tell myself that one fine day *ça va aller* and I will find the ideal job. (Cynthia, 28, graduate in accountancy; Interview March 2014, my translation.)

This catalyst is a momentum of change which gets things going, and it has to be induced by a person's own efforts and desire to change the situation. Some informants, however, add that without good fortune the moment cannot take place. The bridge between the two states – and the conviction that it exists in the first place – seems to be important in order to stay optimistic and continue to struggle. In my interviews, this bridge is in most cases based on hope. During the interviews I asked for an elaboration whenever my interviewee constructed their narration around *ça va aller*. This was the moment when people started to speak of hope and optimism. *Ça va aller* implies dissatisfaction with one's actual situation that stems from the notion that one is temporarily blocked from accessing the goals to which one aspires. The phrase aims at the trigger for when things start to go the way one wants them to go. A firm belief is articulated here that this moment of change is inevitable and not to be questioned; it is less clear, however, when this will become manifest. That notwithstanding, it is this moment upon which all hopes are pinned. One informant underlines that you have to know your position (whether along the intended trajectory or within the social environment) in order to change it – in other words, to start acting towards a moment of change. Therefore, according to informants, one has to be convinced that the moment of change which transforms the now-condition into the afterward-condition is possible. The fact that things will start changing is seen, on the one hand, as a direct consequence of one's efforts combined with good fortune and, on the other hand, as being subject to sudden changes. This is where unpredictability is manifested, and where several strategies have their starting point.

In longer conversations young graduates start sharing other facets of their specific situation, and their self-representation becomes more nuanced. My role during interviews was that of a listener who had never experienced the implications of uncertainty in Burkina Faso; for this reason informants gladly elaborated on what it meant to keep in mind that things would work out alright *(ça va aller)* when the present was structured by the fact that the moment of change was unpredictable. Doubts, complaints and disappointment can be voiced in this context.

My informants' discontent over their situation on the job market is linked to three main aspects: first, the negative conditions of university studies that lead to a diminishing quality in education and result in a lack of experience, which places graduates at a disadvantage in the application process. Many informants claim that they do not feel well-prepared to enter the job market because they lack experience in their fields as a result of the insufficient quality of their studies; this in turn entails not gaining access to jobs and, thus, to a respected status within society. Second, the distribution of jobs is not transparent and, according to my informants, mostly directed by nepotism and patronage. This phenomenon is labelled as »*bras longs*« (long arms). It can be seen as part of what Hyden (1983: 8) describes as the economy of affection: »a network of support, communication and interaction among structurally defined groups connected by blood, kin, community or other affiliations, for example, religion.« My informants claim that the distribution of jobs and internships through *bras longs* leads to a deterioration in the importance of university diplomas for accessing employment. It propels discontent among those graduates who have to struggle with ›short arms‹ due to the fact that they do not come from wealthy, influential families and do not have access to a network during their studies. Third, the government is often criticised for failing to create institutions that support young graduates in becoming independent. My informants express the wish for more funding to start their own businesses, and they criticise that the government's fund for implementing young entrepreneurs' projects is biased and insufficient: »our applications [for funds] will stay on their desks and they will die on their desks.« (Salif, graduate of economics, 30; Interview August 2013; my translation). Those who applied for government funding claim that success is unlikely without an insider at the ministry who can support the application. Others add that even if a project were to be funded, the grant would not suffice to set up a business.

Most of the university graduates in Burkina Faso to whom I have spoken are convinced that the annual recruitment test for the civil service (the *concours*) is the most likely way for them to enter the job market. Only one of the thirty individuals in my research sample never took part in it, and this was because he refused to work for the Burkinabe state. All others compete with tens of thousands of other candidates for a meagre number of jobs. The recruitment tests usually take place in August, and they consist of multiple-choice tests that require general knowledge and logical reasoning; they are completely detached from job-relevant expert knowledge. Preparation classes for the test have become a lucrative business, and workbooks with multiple-choice tests sell well at vending tables. Rumour has it that magical intervention also helps; preparation for the test is a booming business for various types of actors. When the list of offered jobs is released it is spread around within a couple of hours. Deciding in which recruitment tests to participate demands strategy, as some of them are scheduled at the same time. Moreover, there are registration fees to be paid, which restricts most of the participants to a limited selection. Once the tests open for registration, the queues in front of the enrolment sites (for example, the national stadium) spill into the streets. Certain recruitment tests are more popular than others because they promise lucrative posts. Those who are selected are usually announced officially in November. The transition government under Michel Kafando, who succeeded former president Blaise Compaoré following his forced resignation, disrupted this routine in 2015, when they annulled certain results due to fraud – thus confirming suspicions that success in the competition is often linked to cash payments and helpful relationships. Nevertheless, many graduates are convinced that this competition is their only true chance to enter the job market (see Mazzocchetti 2009: 148) and that they hence cannot make use of helpful relations:

Tché! These competitions are difficult! A long time before I finished university I started to participate: last year, the year before that. Well, it is not easy to gain anything there, as the number of vacancies is limited. And there is no inherent logic in the multiple-choice tests, so you need to be lucky. Anyway, we hope to get admitted to the civil service, but it is possible to fail at the competition for two, three, four years after graduation. There are many graduates who tried for four or five years without success. So they don't have a job and they try again each year, but once you are 37 years old you cannot take part in the competition anymore. So you need to succeed by all means before you are 37; if you don't know anybody who can help you to find employment it will be very difficult. (Ada, 29, graduate of law studies; Interview March 2014; my translation.)

My informants make much of the fact that the number of competitors increases each year because past years' failures join the masses of new aspirants. The recruitment tests are a central aspect in many interviews when my informants speak about how they plan their future. Indeed, the tests are seen as the only accessible entry point for popular white-collar jobs. Nevertheless, posts do exists that are rather less attractive, such as those for primary-school teachers in remote areas. These are numerous, but for my informants they are not commensurate with their diploma because the wages are low and the work conditions mostly unfavourable. Only two individuals in my sample decided to take this opportunity, yet both of them see their present teaching activities as temporary in nature. Malik, who participates each year, for example is trying his luck in the recruitment test for the customs service and the ENAREF, like many others from my sample. The likelihood of obtaining a post is fair because the number of participants is greatest there. There are also recruitment tests that are labelled as ›professional‹, which means they do indeed target a specific group, for example the recruitment test for magistrates. Two of my informants who studied computer sciences gained a post in the civil service by participating in a professional recruitment test. All of the law graduates in my sample are taking part in the recruitment test for magistrates, but none of them have been successful yet. Many of those who participate in the tests each year hope that, once they are recruited, they will be able to afford another diploma at university, and some are convinced that they would then start their own business. Most of them are still anticipating the next recruitment test and continue to hope for future success whilst in the meantime sending out applications whenever possible and doing menial jobs or internships. It is precisely in these types of activities that they keep up their hope, as they are convinced that they are just temporal in nature and represent a stepping-stone towards entry into what they see as the ›real‹ job market – be it in the private sector or public administration.

## Outmanoeuvring Unpredictability: Reclaiming the Terrain by Making Hope Work

The way young graduates locate themselves in time as well as in their societal environment is linked to their imagination of a dynamic trajectory, as discussed above in the context of my informants' narrations. In order to show the implications of these dynamics, I will make use of the concept of ›social navigation‹ and the role of hope therein. Vigh (2009: 419) defines social navigation as a concept that is »used when referring to how people act in difficult or uncertain circumstances and in describing how they disentangle themselves from confining structures, plot their escape and move towards better positions.« There is an inherent temporality to the concept of social navigation, because it is constantly adjusted to the present trajectories as well as to the way in which goals are approached. It thus combines present environments and future imaginaries (Vigh 2009: 425) while focusing on the trajectories of individuals. Young graduates also navigate their way through the present by focusing on the objectives they want to reach in the near and far future. I argue that by analysing the dynamics of their present navigation it is possible to retrieve the future through research. In order for graduates to neither lose their orientation (despite sometimes being forced to stray from a straight trajectory) nor to lose their motivation, they make use of hope as a strategy. Interviews quickly showed that hope is a central factor in young graduates' lifeworlds and deeply influences the way in which they navigate towards their objectives. Hope becomes vital especially in regard to the recruitment test, which is the most frequent strategy applied in searching for jobs. There is usually a one-year hiatus between two tests, and it is essential for graduates to sustain the conviction that they will be recruited in the following test. The dynamic aspect of young graduates' life-courses seems to gain its kinetic input less from the passage of time than from an emotional orientation that is best coined as ›hope‹. The emic definition of hope shows that graduates define it as a sort of motor that inspires their acting in the interest of the future. This kinetic aspect becomes apparent when graduates use phrases in their narratives such as »not yet arrived« to describe the fact that they have not yet attained their desired status, or in notions such as »being blocked« when speaking of obstacles that can often lead them to change their routes towards the future:

Sometimes you have the impression that everything is closed. All the doors are closed and no door can be opened. So you are stuck in the middle, surrounded by doors which are closed. Even if you knock at those doors, they are not going to open. [...] That gives you the impression that you are not moving. We [the young graduates] are not moving. It is said that if you do not move, you are going backwards. If you do not advance and you are stuck like that, you know that you are going backwards and time is leaving you behind. (Pascal, 30, graduate of sociology; Interview February 2014, my translation.)

The notion of individuals moving – or navigating – through time towards their objectives becomes evident in Pascal's narrations, and so does the idea of being stuck while time passes. It is seen as a person's own responsibility to disentangle themselves from this unfavourable state so as to be able to continue navigating and acting towards their goals. This is where hope becomes important and is expressed in the interviews I have conducted. Early interviews were full of references to hope; therefore, in consecutive interviews I inquired into the emic meaning of hope. It quickly became clear that young graduates actively work with their hopes in order to unblock the future to which they aspire. They create hopeful moments in the sense of practices that nurture their hope and enable them to hold onto it by creating the possibility for change. Hope propels the actions and informs the imaginaries of these young graduates and is deeply entangled with practices that can thus be seen as an important component in the framing concept of social navigation. This is borne out by other research that inquires into the link between hope and agency. Bjarnesen's (2009: 121) ethnographic work on young Ivorian migrants considers the concept of hope to be more suitable for capturing the uncertainty that characterises anticipations than the notions of aspirations and agency, »which tend to emphasize the capacity of the individual to steer a course through life; to envision a future and act in order to make it happen. As such, an attention to hope might better combine the active aspirations and practices of the hoper with the social forces that are seen to influence the possible or past outcomes of specific hopes.« Turner (2015: 180) describes how hope informs the way in which young Burundian refugees in Nairobi »navigate in the present in order to increase [their] odds for a better future«, as well as inspiring action that aims to change the future. In his profound ethnography on young, unemployed men in Ethiopia, Mains (2012) inquires into their struggle to attain their hopes for the future whilst constantly threatened by the lack of opportunities that youths in Ethiopia face. Sliwinski (2012) analyses hope as a category that is relevant to agency when she discusses how hope and value are combined in the post-disaster humanitarian context of El Salvador; similar to the case in Burkina Faso, here hope is defined as a ›modality of doing‹ when future-oriented practices are grounded in hope. Giraud (2007) highlights the way in which hope influences practices by operationalising it as a category for analysing actions. Like this he shows that hope can serve as a motor for actions as well as being mobilised by action; hence, it is characterised by its dynamic aspect. Hope in Burkinabe graduates displays the same attributes, as I will now show by drawing on data from my field research. I argue that hope and agency are intertwined in the case of Burkinabe graduates because they clearly inform each other – and especially because graduates see themselves as capable of actively working towards a better future. Hope sets them in motion and makes them follow their routes, in the sense of stimulus as well as navigation instrument. During interviews and conversations it became clear that hope is not linked to ›waithood‹ (Honwana 2012) in a deterministic sense but instead to individual action.

Therefore it is described as a positive attitude to the future that requires specific types of maintenance, as Liliane formulates for us:

In my opinion, hope means thinking that everything is going to be fine, it means thinking that tomorrow I can have what I can't have today, why not? So this is what hope means for me. That I don't sit down, inevitably saying that I will never succeed. Instead, it means maintaining the idea that even if I don't succeed today, I can succeed tomorrow. [...] In my personal opinion, as I am religious and believe in God, I think that the basis for hope is the conviction that God will do something for me. Even if this is not now, in favourable times things will work better for me. So, first, there is the belief, and second there is the contribution of one's competence and talents. (Liliane, 28, graduate of law studies; Interview February 2014, my translation.)

She mentions two important foundations for hope: individual competence and talents on the one hand and, on the other hand, the belief in God. Other informants outline determination, courage and individual skills as further prerequisites for hope. But whereas those prerequisites themselves already demand a strong will and a positive attitude towards the future, one has to act upon hope in order to make it work:

Hope is the certainty of a better tomorrow, it is the conviction of a better tomorrow, and it is this certainty and conviction which allows you to act, because if you have no hope you are trapped in a maelstrom of despair where you don't act – and if you don't act, you don't evolve; and if you don't evolve, you are sad. But if you have hope, you struggle by telling yourself that the next days or months will be better than the present. So hope allows you to move from a situation ›x‹, which is not favourable, to a situation ›y‹ in the near-or-far future which is more favourable. (Elise, 29, medical doctor; Interview March 2014, my translation.)

Hope requires investment and allows people to act towards the future, as Elise stresses when she illustrates ›hope‹ as a facilitator for individuals to evolve and follow their ambitions. Another informant explains that hope enables desirable change to be realised: his dreams and the imagination of his satisfaction once he obtains his goals motivate him to augment his chances of making them into reality. Hopelessness is seen as defeat, and although some of my informants acknowledge that, from time to time, they lose hope because of the hardship they experience, they nevertheless insist that these are occasional periods – comparable to the doldrums at sea, to stick with the metaphor of navigation – which they overcome with the help of their families and their belief in God. In fact, doubts, fears and hopelessness are expressed during many interviews, yet these are temporary in character. Augustin is illustrative of this:

Only those who do not have an objective lose their hope definitely, because when you have an objective, you struggle. You see what you have to do. So whenever there is the possibility to do something it will always help you for the future. (Augustin, 31, graduate of law studies; Interview May 2014, my translation.)

These kinds of narrations suggest a sense of acting and of individual responsibility for one's trajectory, and they are commonly heard during interviews on future perspectives. Ousmane, a graduate in economics, stresses that it is hope which allows him to project himself into the future, and therefore it is a way for him to enter the future in pursuit of his goals. Hope is seen as a resource for action and for navigating through terrain littered by contemporary obstacles; yet at the same time it requires investments in the sense of effort, as Madi explains:

I think that hope is hidden behind all of our present activities. We do not work in order to sit at home one day in the future. We study with the objective of acquiring something, and it is this ambition of acquiring something later on that is in our heads; and I call that hope. (Madi, 28, graduate of accountancy; Interview April 2014, my translation.)

Hope allows individuals to transform unfavourable situations into stepping-stones, or necessary detours, that lead to intended goals in the future. Pascal (a sociology graduate) answers the initial question of what he is presently doing with: »presently, I am not doing anything [...] but ça va aller.« Later on, however, he explains that he is spending most of the time in a consultation office, where he does different tasks without being properly paid – but he sees profit for his future in this activity, not only because he is gaining experience in social research but also because he can greatly expand his networks. Similarly, most of my informants do work, even if this is not in their field of study and in most cases is either not remunerated at all or only pays a miniscule wage. This applies, for example, to Cynthia, who studied accountancy and has worked as a promoter for a mayonnaise brand ever since her graduation three years ago, but who nevertheless clings to her goal of creating a staffing firm one day. Or to Abdul, a graduate of psychology, who accepted a short-term contract as a philosophy teacher in a remote province, but who still maintains his ambition of working with an NGO where he could apply his training as a psychologist. Many graduates who are now in a job unrelated to their ambitions plan to invest their salary in additional diplomas, which are still seen as gate-openers on the job market. Some of my informants have already started further studies at private universities, and one of them continued on to a Master's programme at the public university of Ouagadougou. They call the motivation for these activities ›hope‹, and it is hope that allows them to transform what may have been regarded as failure (from the point of view of projecting the future during their studies) into the initial push in the direction of an intended trajectory.

Living and working on one's faith, mostly by praying regularly, fasting and attending church or mosque services, represents an important investment in hope and is seen as working on one's good fortune. The belief in God's benevolence is connected to the actions that must be taken so as to prevent God from forgetting about a person's need for His help. It involves the notion that as long as a person tries by all means to improve his or her situation, God will intervene for an improvement. This approach also serves as an explanation for the successes of others. Counting on God is not a form of fatalism but of agency, because in order to retain faith in a better future a person needs to apply their talents and the belief in Gods benevolence, which will become manifest through good fortune:

Hope is important but you have to associate it with fortune because the foundation of hope must be effort. I know that I will struggle, and so I have hope that I will be alright while struggling. It is possible that my efforts alone will not be enough; I also need to have good fortune. Hope and fortune have to happen together, and if you experience failure, it might be linked to a lack of good fortune. But if you do not struggle, you will not succeed. You can even be fortunate; but as long as you are not struggling, you will not gain anything. If I just sit here I might get lucky, but luck will not descend towards me and find me. But if I work towards it, it can facilitate opportunities for me. (Ahmed, 29, graduate of economics; Interview May 2014, my translation.)

The idea that God distributes good fortune is common amongst my informants and implies a kind of reciprocal agency. This connects to the initial idea of university degrees as fundamental gate-openers to a better future. Once arriving at a point where a change for the better becomes possible, diplomas are imagined to be facilitators. Yet, to reach these points one must continue to head forwards despite the unpredictability that has to be managed; and hope is a fundamental element in this kind of acting towards the future in the case of the Burkinabe graduates. Hope as presented by my informants is central to the way in which they navigate towards their goals, because it allows them to act despite the unpredictability they presently face. Like this they become able to keep their objectives in sight, even if these are regularly transformed and adjusted over time. Because hope has to be maintained constantly, it is itself a type of strategy when working towards the future.

## Conclusion

Researching the future has to rely on inquiring into the present practices of individuals. The practices of Burkinabe graduates are deeply entangled with their aspired futures, and informants outline this connection when speaking about their present situation. Usually, the point of reference is the future, and they value their status in relation to what they hope their status to be in the future. Drawing on the insights from interviews and the everyday practices of young graduates, hope can be seen as facilitating agency in regard to accomplishing goals. When projecting their trajectories across the terrain (or contexts of action) contoured by their social situation, the narration recurs on the individual's trajectory, thereby connecting the discourse of hope with the notion of agency. Their practices reflect the fact that while they may be trapped in an unfavourable situation, they nevertheless have ideas on how to extricate themselves and advance in order to approach their goals. Hope allows graduates to anticipate and work towards a favourable future in which they will attain their goals, even if they could appear to be headed in the wrong direction in the present. Thus, Burkinabe graduates act towards a future that is far more than merely a vague notion of a better tomorrow for them. They are far from being fatalistic; they do drift in a terrain informed by uncertainty. On the contrary, their imagination allows them to focus on their ambitions at the same time as their practices, informed through hope, continue to take aim at them. They are navigators who constantly face challenges due to their uncertain situation, but who nevertheless are convinced of being headed in the right direction, specifically the direction that allows them eventually to access their future goals. Yet in order to keep up this attitude, they must continue to act. In this they share common terrain, but their trajectories differ, even if they are often inspired by the promising strategies of others. This notwithstanding, their goals are almost equivalent and unchanging, even if in many cases the expected moment of arrival has had to be postponed. During the three-year period of my field research, some of my informants moved to other towns, some got married, others divorced, some had children, some started new jobs or lost old ones. Nevertheless, their aspirations stayed mostly the same. And often they transformed what had earlier been seen as a goal into a new stepping-stone once it had been reached.

## BIBLIOGRAPHY

Bjarnesen, Jesper. 2009. »A Mobile Life Story. Tracing Hopefulness in the Life and Dreams of a Young Ivorian Migrant.« *Migration Letters* 6(2): 119-129.

Giraud, Claude. 2007. *De L'Espoir*. Paris: Harmattan.

Honwana, Alcinda. 2012. *The Time of Youth. Work, Social Change, and Politics in Africa*. Boulder and London: Kumarian Press.

Hyden, Goran. 1983. *No Shortcuts to Progress: African Development Management in Perspective*. Berkeley: University of California Press.

Jackson, Michael. 1998. *Minima Ethnographica: Intersubjectivity and the Anthropological Subject*. Chicago: University of Chicago Press.

Mains, Daniel. 2012. *Hope is Cut. Youth, Unemployment, and the Future in Urban Ethiopia*. Philadelphia: Temple University Press.

Mazzocchetti, Jacinthe. 2009. *Etre étudiant à Ouagadougou. Itinérances, imaginaire et précarité*. Paris: Karthala.

Sliwinski, Alicia. 2012. »Working Hope: Around Labour and Value in a Humanitarian Context.« *Anthropologica* 54(2): 227-238.

Turner, Simon. 2015. »›We wait for miracles.‹ Ideas of Hope and Future among Clandestine Burundian Refugees in Nairobi.« In *Ethnographies of Uncertainty in Africa*, edited by Elizabeth Cooper and David Pratten. Basingstoke: Palgrave Macmillan. 173-192.

Vigh, Henrik. 2009. »Motion Squared: A Second Look at the Concept of Social Navigation.« *Anthropological Theory*, 9(4): 419-438.

# 4 ›Opening up *La Chance*‹
## (Un)certainty among University Graduates in Bamako, Mali

Susann Ludwig

## INTRODUCTION

With a public university campus, four state-run Institutes of Higher Education and numerous private universities, Bamako is clearly Mali's centre of higher education. In 2010, about 70,000 students were enrolled at the University of Bamako; every year, more than 10,000 graduate. They grew up in the belief that studying is a privilege, and they were promised that education would guarantee employment and, therefore, a livelihood. Until the 1980s university degrees secured access to public-sector employment; thus, their parents' generation experienced the fulfilment of that promise. But Mali's public sector has been saturated for years and the country's economy is still predominantly based on agriculture. In other words, today's reality is dramatically different for graduates. Although less than two per cent of the Malian population hold a university degree, graduates still constitute the country's educational elite and, yet, it is this group that is most affected by unemployment. They are losing the advantage of their privilege. Not only have the future benefits of higher education been lost, but also the quality of higher education itself is in doubt.

Today more than 70 per cent of young academics in Mali are searching for employment (APEJ 2011). They encounter severe difficulties in finding a job that corresponds to their qualifications, and it is a challenge for them to enter the labour market at all. Secure employment ensures secure futures, people say. Since there is no secure employment in the present, the present is uncertain and, therefore, so is the future. University graduates find themselves in situations characterised by uncertainty, which affects not only how they imagine and plan their futures but also their actions in the present.

In response to that, I argue, Malian graduates ›open up *la chance*‹. *La chance* separates the present from the future since it enables a different present – something that has been imagined as the future in the past. University graduates in Mali create *la chance* (opportunities); they take *la chance* (chances), but they also happen to have *la chance* (serendipity) or simply get *la chance* (good fortune). »God provides *la chance*, but you're able to open up *la chance* on your own, too,« an informant explained. *La chance* is ambiguous: it can be accessed and influenced by individual action, but it is also believed to be God's will, which cannot be enforced.

This is a similar response to what Johnson-Hanks (2005: 363) has conceptualised as ›judicious opportunism‹, meaning that »the actor seizes promising chances.« Johnson-Hanks conducted ethnographic research among young educated Beti women in Cameroon, who shared their ideas on marriage and reproduction with her. By connecting these ideas with a theoretical analysis of intentional action, she claims that Beti women are aware of the uncertainty of the future. In response they do not pursue fixed plans but instead adapt to opportunities as they appear. Her main argument elaborates on the relationship between intention, action and outcome in contexts characterised by uncertainty. She concludes that ›judicious opportunism‹ is the most flexible and, hence, the best strategy within that framework (ibid.: 377). As much as I agree with her argument, her paper does not sufficiently deal with questions such as what it is that people actually do or, more specifically, how they create certainty through present-day action that is geared towards the future. I will engage with these questions by introducing the process of ›opening up *la chance*‹, which is about ›seizing opportunities‹ or identifying *la chance*, but also about preparing and transforming it.

This contribution focuses on narratives of individual and common experiences with *la chance* – a phenomenon perceived as the key to enabling futures; it does not focus on individual biographies and futures. In order to systematise and ultimately capture the abstract and complex phenomenon of *la chance*, I outline a typology of *la chance*. Based on the application of ethnomethodology's Membership Categorization Analysis to narrative interviews, I present three types of *la chance*: prerequisites, sprouts and outcomes. These are connected to each other through actions taken by individual during the process of ›opening up *la chance*‹ (*ouvrir la chance*). This process again consists of three essential parts: looking for *la chance* (preparation), finding *la chance* (identification), and working with *la chance* (transformation).

Furthermore, this paper demonstrates that *la chance* enables specific futures. *La chance* is exclusive; it suddenly appears and needs to be identified by a prepared individual. It is ultimately argued that the process of ›opening up *la chance*‹ is a way of dealing with uncertainty in the present and, consequently, a way to access the future.

## Methodology

This paper is based on a total of nine months of fieldwork between 2013 and 2015 in Bamako, Mali, which I conducted in the context of my PhD studies. Three samples of narrative interviews were conducted with thirty young academics (ten female, twenty male). The longitudinal character of the study should enable us to understand not only the informants' social context but also how university graduates construct their futures in the present. No one has privileged access to the future; and the future is uncertain. However, there are ways of accessing the future with reference to present social practices. The idea of ›opening up *la chance*‹ points to such practices.

In order to approach the notion of *la chance* in the interviews, I looked at the various contexts in which informants talked about it. The term is mentioned in three different contexts: first, in fixed expressions such as *bonne chance* or *tenter la chance*. The second centres on the description of what *la chance* is, either the abstract *avoir l'opportunité de faire qc* or the concrete *travailler dans les ONGs* or *faire un stage*. *La chance* generally is ›to do something‹, whether it is professional (to create, manage, realise) or non-professional (to live, love, play), but it is also ›to have‹ (a diploma, an opportunity, employment) or ›to be something‹ (chosen, lucky, accepted). The third context in which *la chance* is mentioned problematises how it can be accessed, which is either in an active manner, as in *se battre* (to fight), *prendre ta vie en main* (to take control of one's destiny) or passively, as in *Dieu donne la chance* (God gives *la chance*).

For this article, I have selected extracts from interviews of the third sample, which was generated in 2015. These extracts focus on *la chance*

– an emic concept that turned out to be crucial already in earlier stages of my research. I asked questions like: What is *la chance*? What does *la chance* mean to you? Could you identify moments in your life in which you encountered *la chance*? Following this, I conducted analytical free-writing on these interview passages, describing what these extracts' themes, which helped me to gain a better understanding of what university graduates mean when they refer to *la chance*.

In order to describe the phenomenon of *la chance*, I took up *An Invitation to Ethnomethodology* (Francis and Hester 2004) and conducted Membership Categorisation Analysis (MCA), which »is concerned with the organization of common-sense knowledge in terms of the categories members employ in accomplishing their activities in and through talk« (ibid.: 21).

MCA is about the identification of membership categorisation devices, which are a collection of membership categories and their rules of application. Here is a popular example (Stokoe 2012: 281): »The baby cries. The mother picks it up.« The ›baby‹ and the ›mother‹ are so-called categories. Now, there are rules of application such as category-bound activities, which refer to activities connected with a category, for example, ›crying‹ as a category-bound activity of the ›baby‹ or ›picking up‹ for the ›mother‹. In other words, category-bound activities give information about what it is that a certain category (›baby‹, ›mother‹) does. Another rule of application that is pertinent to this case is that of category-tied predicates, which refer to characteristics connected with a category, for example, ›demanding‹ as a category-tied predicate of the ›baby‹, or ›caring‹ for the ›mother‹ (see also Francis and Hester 2004; Silverman 1998; Stokoe 2012; Ten Have 2004).

To return to the example of »the baby cried; the mother picked it up.« There is nothing strange about this phrase. Vice versa, this would seem irritating: »The mother cried; the baby picked it up.« When it comes to the phenomenon of *la chance*, however, both stories are accurate: »*La chance* cried. The graduate picked it up.« (In other words, *la chance* appeared and the graduate took it.) And vice versa: »The graduate cried. *La chance* picked her/him up.« (The graduate was searching and *la chance* appeared.)

However, the relation between *la chance* and graduate presents itself as ambiguous. ›La chance‹ and ›graduate‹ constitute a pair. But it is not a unique pair: ›la chance‹ is not constituted by ›graduate‹, and ›graduate‹ does not constitute ›la chance‹. *La chance* exists without the graduate, and the graduate still exists without *la chance*. However, the relationship between the two is crucial because ›la chance‹ defines ›graduate‹, and ›graduate‹ identifies ›la chance‹. This article focuses on that relationship since it demonstrates how graduates experience *la chance* and what it is that they do with *la chance*.

MCA was a useful tool for me to disentangle the ambiguous nature of *la chance* by, first, itemising informants' common-sense meanings of *la chance* and second, systematising different types of *la chance*. Rather than members' descriptions of persons (e.g. ›baby‹, ›mother‹), I was interested in their descriptions of a phenomenon – specifically, university graduates' descriptions of *la chance*. Therefore, I considered what university graduates referred to as *la chance* as a collective category for MCA. This was followed by analysing *la chance* as a category in terms of category-bound activities and category-tied predicates of *la chance*. I discovered that the emic term ›la chance‹ is a category which consists of several types I will refer to below as ›prerequisites‹, ›sprouts‹ and ›outcomes‹. These three types of *la chance* are interconnected through practices of ›opening up *la chance*‹ (›looking for *la chance*‹, ›finding *la chance*‹, ›working with *la chance*‹). The ultimate result of this analysis is a typology of *la chance*, which I now proceed to introduce in the following section. This will permit a more systematic understanding of what *la chance* is for university graduates in Bamako, what it does to them, as well as how they ›open up *la chance*‹.

## Exploring *LA CHANCE*

The university graduates I met in Bamako are working on the realisation of their futures – some of them have already achieved their goals, and some have not (yet). If it is personal effort which they all invest, what is it that, from their perspective, makes the difference? *La chance* makes a difference. It is distinctive, and it distinguishes. *La chance* is considered to determine the future outcome of graduates' present actions. Everyone is looking for *la chance*, yet it is not there for everyone. For university graduates the notion of *la chance* is a way of answering the puzzling question of why some people make it whereas some do not.

Malian graduates reflected on *la chance* either retrospectively or with reference to the future, but it is in the present that they work on increasing their exposure to it. As long as things stay the same, the future has not yet arrived. In other words, *la chance* with a future perspective is a well-defined moment: it is the point in time when their efforts are rewarded.

There are three different types of *la chance*: prerequisites, sprouts and outcomes. These types are connected through the practice of ›opening up *la chance*‹, which itself consists of three practices: ›looking for *la chance*‹, ›finding *la chance*‹ and ›working with *la chance*‹. One type of *la chance* might add up to, or turn into, another type through practices of ›opening up *la chance*‹. It can be understood as akin to a chain, which has a beginning but no definite end. The following part of my contribution gives a detailed account of this typology of *la chance*. I begin by introducing prerequisites as the preconditions of the process of ›opening up *la chance*‹, which will then be discussed in the subsequent section.

## Prerequisites: Possession

In order to discover what *la chance* is, I coded the interview extracts in terms of category-tied predicates (which are included in footnotes here). This allowed me to identify three different types of *la chance*. The first type is what I call ›prerequisites‹. These prerequisites constitute the context into which individuals are born and socialised (e.g. family, environment, education). They are often referred to as *ma chance* (my chance) – *la chance* in possession. Prerequisites are *la chance* that has not been opened up by an individual but, instead, has been open to the individual from the very beginning. Most graduates considered these to be privileges. Prerequisites constitute a starting point that appears to be distributed randomly – a distinguishing factor that also enables further *la chance*.

University graduates do not consider this type of *la chance* as their personal achievement; rather, they are already equipped with it. In most cases, prerequisites are attributed to an external force such as God or coincidence. The following example demonstrates a clear distinction between the two: God is religion, but coincidence is something different. However, both provide *la chance*.

SL: Do you think that God made us meet in the first place?
A: Ah, no. That was a coincidence. You know, if we talk about God here, it is all about religion. But this is really a coincidence. So, the fact that we were almost neighbours. It's a coincidence that we met. [...] Human beings are shaped by their environment. So, I'd say that it is the environment. There are areas in Bamako

where you'd never meet a white person. And yeah, that was ma chance. (Interview 2015 with Siaka, 29, English graduate; my translation.)[1]

Siaka, my field assistant, described the fact that we met as *la chance* because it later led to employment for him. He argues for the importance of context when it comes to *la chance*. Living in the same area and getting to know each other are coincidences. He did not do anything to bring it about, and he was not living there in order to look for *la chance*. But living in the right area makes it more likely to find *la chance* even if one is not looking for it. For him, the area he lives in is a prerequisite. This is *la chance* in the sense that it preconditioned us meeting each other. In other words, coincidence is *la chance*.

*La chance* as a prerequisite is an individual's foundation for looking for further *la chance*, in a similar way as a gardener inspects the soil where she has planted seeds. Prerequisites define the starting point in the process of ›opening up *la chance*‹. Graduates are aware of the privilege of their education:

Going to school as a kid was ma chance to me. There are a lot of girls and also boys that do not have this la chance and they are on the streets today. [...] It's because their parents did not have the means to send them to school. [...] I'd say school is la chance for me: being literate, being intellectual. That is la chance. Not everyone is an intellectual, because not everyone had la chance to go to school. (Interview 2015 with Rokiatou, 32, sociology graduate; my translation.)[2]

There are many children who do not go to school, either because their parents' financial situation precluded it or because they had other plans for their children. In other words, being born into a family with both the attitude towards and the financial means for their children's studies is *la chance*, and so is education itself. Graduating from university, ›being an intellectual‹ is *la chance*. One of the reasons for this lies in the fact that only few individuals graduate; they are an exception and constitute the educated elite. For Simone *la chance* is something that made her exceptional as well:

---

[1] | Code: la_chance\category-tied_predicate\environment\prerequisite.
[2] | Code: la_chance\ category-tied_predicate\means\prerequisite.

I've had la chance to travel. No one in my family had la chance to travel abroad before. I did my university degree [Master's] abroad. I thank God for that. I also never thought of integrating professionally as quickly as I did. That was la chance. [...] I also had la chance to have wonderful parents. I grew up in a family with different religious beliefs in harmony. I have a lot of la chance. [...] I have la chance to be healthy. (Interview 2015 with Simone, 24, law-school graduate; my translation.)[3]

Simone was the first person in her family to travel and study abroad – that is *la chance*. She is grateful for that opportunity, which has made her biography unique amongst her relatives as well as in comparison to the rest of Malian society. Ultimately, this puts her in a privileged position on the labour market when looking for *la chance*. Simone lists numerous examples of what *la chance* is to her: her opportunities, her job, her family and her health. There are a wide range of things she is thankful for, and she recognises them as privileges that were preconditioned by her birth or by an outside force. For Simone, *la chance* is her family; for Oumar, it is friendship:

O: I've always met amazing people throughout my life. I consider that to be la chance. But it wasn't me who provoked it. [...]
SL: So, receiving your job is not?
O: No, no. [...] It's because of Adama that I got that job today. So, la chance that I have is to have Adama as a friend. At university, it was the same. He often paid for my transport to school because I couldn't afford it. [...] It is la chance that I met him and the reason why I am where I am today. (Interview 2015 with Oumar, 27, economics graduate; my translation.)[4]

For Oumar *la chance* is primarily his friendship with Adama. He emphasises that he did not provoke that. It has never been his intention to make friends in order to benefit from them in any financial or professional sense. Oumar has not been calculative; he did not anticipate any advantages when he first met Adama. This is basically why he believes in *la chance* – *la chance* is something with which he was provided. Oumar attributes the fact that he was able to finish his studies and find employment to

---

3 | Code: la_chance\ category-tied_predicate\privilege\prerequisite.
4 | Code: la_chance\ category-tied_predicate\friendship\prerequisite.

his friend Adama, who has always been supportive of him. In this case, friendship is the prerequisite for access to a job and money.

To sum up, environment, family and friends, and related opportunities are *la chance* in the sense of prerequisites. They compose an individual's point of departure for the process of ›opening up *la chance*‹, which I will now discuss.

## ›Opening up *la chance*‹

›Opening up *la chance*‹ (*ouvrir la chance*) is a process of action that is directed towards the future. This process consists of three connected practices: ›looking for *la chance*‹ (*chercher la chance*) or preparation, ›finding *la chance*‹ (*trouver la chance*) or identification, and ›working with *la chance*‹ (*bénéficier de la chance*) or transformation. To look for *la chance* means to prepare in order to be able to create or identify *la chance* when it appears and, then, to transform *la chance* into a state of possession. With the help of interview extracts I coded as graduates' category-bound activities in relation to *la chance*, the following section highlights how university graduates talk about their engagement in these practices in the process of ›opening up *la chance*‹.

### Looking for *la chance:* Preparation

University graduates do not simply receive *la chance*, but they are ›looking for‹ or provoking *la chance* as a means of preparing for its appearance. They are preparing not because *la chance* is guaranteed to emerge like a sprout from the soil, but because graduates are convinced that they will eventually find it. However, *la chance* is not only about getting or finding it but also about preparing for it, as the next interview excerpt demonstrates:

> La chance exists, but in my life there is not a lot of it. We say that if you look for la chance, you'll find la chance. But if you don't look for it, you cannot speak of la chance. (Interview 2015 with Siaka, 29, English graduate; my translation.)[5]

Siaka distinguishes between *la chance* in general and in his life. He has not experienced much *la chance*; yet, he is convinced of its existence. He knows that it is only by looking for *la chance* that one will find it. It is

---

5 | Code: la_chance\category-bound_activity\opening_up\looking_for.

the practice of ›looking for‹ that defines *la chance*. To put it differently, *la chance* is the result of practices of ›looking for‹. It is only *la chance* if it has been looked for in the first place. Things that simply happen are therefore not *la chance*. In other words, there is a difference between ›looking for‹ and ›finding‹ *la chance*. It does exist, but only those who look for it will be able to find it.

Let's take soccer as an example: if you want to have la chance to score, you need to know how to play first. So, it is in this sense that you can provoke la chance. In real life, you need la chance to have a good job and for that you first need a good diploma . [...] So, in this sense you can provoke la chance, but la chance could also show up just like that. For example, when I met Adama. (Interview 2015 with Oumar, 27, economics graduate; my translation.)[6]

Oumar provides soccer as an example: scoring is *la chance*, and if you want to score you must know how to play the game. Conversely, if you are not fit and are neither able to dribble the ball nor understand the game, then you cannot score. Figuratively speaking, there are skills required in order to open up *la chance*; and these skills are informed by preparation and practice. »In real life, *la chance* is to have a job,« Oumar says. If you want *la chance* of being employed, you have to be qualified and well-educated. Again, there is no guarantee that there will be *la chance* – neither in soccer nor in real life. However, mastering the game of soccer or holding a university degree renders individuals capable of provoking *la chance* and, therefore, makes them more likely to receive *la chance*. To provoke *la chance* is to look for *la chance* in the sense that individuals provide themselves with the set of skills necessary for them to be able to identify *la chance* when it appears.

But there is also another *la chance*, one which appears »just like that«. Oumar connects this type of *la chance* with his friendship to Adama. To him, friendship is *la chance*. He did not provoke it – it simply ›is‹. There is no rule for meeting great people. »We met just like that and we became friends just like that.« Friendship, it seems, cannot be provoked, but only fostered. Oumar appreciates their friendship for everything that it is. His employment opportunity was unexpected, and it is true that while it

---

**6** | Code: la_chance\category-bound_activity\opening_up\preparation\looking_for.

originated in that friendship, it did not grow out of that friendship. Oumar did not establish his relationship with Adama with the intention of finding employment. Nevertheless, Oumar found *la chance* without having genuinely looked for it. The intention to provoke *la chance* is beyond the scope of intention in friendships. When it shows up through friendship, it comes as a surprise and it is experienced as having ›just happened‹.

Rokiatou, in contrast, describes how she seeks *la chance* by creating and using professional networks based on an anticipated outcome. She builds relationships with people working in her field or who are themselves well-connected. »If someone working for an interesting company lived next-door, I would surely get in touch with that person: present myself, my qualifications and my professional goals,« she explained. In case that person knew of a job offer, he or she would then think of Rokiatou. »You have to be courageous and keep on looking and maybe *la chance* will nurture you one day,« she says, recognising that there is no guarantee that *la chance* would appear. Consequently, efforts made in looking for *la chance* are more like promising ventures than secure investments.

Madou looked for *la chance*, too – in multiple directions. His dream was to become a researcher. »The company I'm working for? I did not choose it,« he says. He always admired those people in their fancy cars and clothes, but he never intended to work for them. »Never,« he emphasises. Madou acquired his diploma in 2010 but was unable to find a job quickly. His mother suggested that he should talk to his uncle, who held a high position at a telecommunications company.

For a whole year [...] I passed by my uncle's house to ask about an internship. ›Could you get me an internship?‹ He'd say: ›Yeah, come back here tomorrow,‹ and I came back the next day. I did that for a whole year. So I became discouraged. My mother always told me: ›Go there again.‹ [...] And one day, he talked to my boss: ›We need to take that kid as an intern. He is really starting to bother me.‹ He said: ›Okay. Let's take him as a commercial agent.‹ (Interview 2015 with Madou, 27, physics graduate; my translation.)[7]

His persistent efforts were not directed towards his initial professional destination but to an alternative, similarly difficult goal. Although he did

---

7 | Code: la_chance\category-bound_activity\opening_up\persistence\looking_for.

not envision a future as a commercial agent, he did perceive his uncle as a possible gate-opener to employment in general. Madou considers this first internship at a telecommunication company as *la chance*. He recognises his own persistence and says, at the same time, that he had no influence on the matter since it was his uncle who had to ask and his boss who decided.

Again, *la chance* is the result of a combination of prerequisites and practices of looking for *la chance*. These practices are characterised by anticipation and commitment; their core lies in preparation. Graduates prepare in order to make sure they are able to find *la chance* when it appears. The appearance of *la chance* and its identification by graduates is an interplay that will now be presented.

## A sprout appears: Identifying *la chance*

This part of my contribution introduces what I have coded as the category-bound activity of ›finding *la chance*‹ and the category-tied predicate of ›sprout‹. This second type of *la chance*, which I call a ›sprout‹ in the sense of a sprouting plant, and the practice of ›opening up *la chance*‹ are closely connected. The sprouting of *la chance* is the key here: provided that this sprout appears and is identified as such by an individual, the future will work out well.

Some informants referred to the following type of *la chance* as ›a sprout‹ that suddenly appears. I like this metaphor because it conveys the sense that ›opening up *la chance*‹ is like the planting of seeds: university graduates are the ones who plant, but the seeds themselves need to grow as well. When a sprout appears, it does not show up in a flash and a bang. It is small and fragile and can therefore easily be overlooked by people who previously did not sow any seeds. But those who do see a sprout must still take good care for it to flourish. University graduates refer to it in real life as an opportunity or coincidence. This sprout itself cannot be created by individuals, however. Its actual emergence is beyond an individual's influence, but an individual is required for it to be recognised. To put this differently, a sprout of *la chance* needs to be identified by an individual who is prepared. Siaka knows what he wants and executes his decisions accordingly:

Yeah, I've always said that I had la chance with my friends, because I chose them. [...] La chance originates in the person itself; you have to choose what you want.

But I think it's difficult to choose because choices fall as they will like that. And you have to know what you want. This is how you'll find la chance. (Interview 2015 with Siaka, 29, English graduate; my translation.)[8]

He emphasises that *la chance* is a product of human reasoning and, therefore, of human action. Decisions, if they are directed towards a fixed goal, will lead to *la chance*. Siaka is focused and able to prioritise different options and identify *la chance*. Simone argues along the same lines:

I tell myself I already have some [professional] experience and I know that I can get there. If you know what you want and you are willing to work hard for it, God will help you to get there for sure. God is going to provide me with la chance to succeed, because I know what I want and I'll work hard for that. So, the two complement each other. (Interview 2015 with Simone, 24, law-school graduate; my translation.)[9]

For her *la chance* is the result of both goal-oriented hard work and God's blessing. Simone already knows her way and it is this knowledge that enables her to identify God's provision of *la chance*. Knowing what you want is presented here as the key criterion to *la chance* in the sense of an initial sprout. Such sprouts create differences; they privilege some people while leaving others with what is considered to be normality:

There were a lot of other interns, more than twenty, but we were the only ones who were allowed to produce our own reports. That was la chance. [...] The others were also upright and hard-working. I don't know, but I believe it's like an impulse for something to flourish. La chance is a sprout. It's true that we've contributed to it, but it was also la chance itself. (Interview 2015 with Simone, 24, law-school graduate; my translation.)[10]

There were many interns, but only Simone and her friend worked on their own reports. *La chance* distinguishes. It is because an identified norm exists that *la chance* is recognised. *La chance* exists in relation to the norm; it is exceptional. Simone explains that she does not differ from others

---

**8** | Code: la_chance\category-bound_activity\opening_up\decision\finding.
**9** | Code: la_chance\category-bound_activity\opening_up\conviction\finding.
**10** | Code: la_chance\category-tied_predicate\impulse\sprout.

who work as interns, but it was she and her friend who received *la chance*; it was she who became the exception. From this perspective, people are not perceived to be different, but it is *la chance* that creates difference. *La chance* in this sense is like a sprout that enables something new, or as Simone formulates: »*La chance* is like an impulse for something to flourish.« For Simone it is *la chance* that made her become the exception. Siaka, in contrast, argues for his own capacities that qualified him for *la chance*:

La chance is also within human beings. What I'm saying is that humans come with all their capacities to the game of la chance. When I saw you, I came closer, I talked to you; but how many people have seen you, too, and simply passed on by? I talked to you, we got to know each other and as soon as you had something... BAM! You gave me the opportunity. You think you would have given me the job if I hadn't talked to you in the first place? It's like that. (Interview 2015 with Siaka, 29, English graduate; my translation.)[11]

Siaka easily interacts and connects with people. He initiated a conversation with me whereas many others living in our neighbourhood did not. If he had not approached me, this job opportunity might not have shown up. It was his qualification in combination with his behaviour that distinguished him from others and, »BAM«, there was *la chance*, there was the sprout he was looking for:

You needed someone to transcribe those interviews. That was la chance for me. You knew me already. That was an advantage. You did not know anyone else for that; and then, simple as that, you took me. (Interview 2015 with Siaka, 29, English graduate; my translation.)[12]

My need to find someone to help with interview transcriptions appeared as Siaka's *la chance*, he says. It is pertinent to note that he depicts this sprout as *la chance* to him, whereas it was »simple as that« to me. Even though he acknowledges that I was looking for someone to assist me, he does not speculate that knowing him might have been *la chance* to me, too. Obviously, *la chance* is a matter of perspective. Siaka's conception of

---

**11** | Code: la_chance\category-tied_predicate\opportunity\sprout.
**12** | Code: la_chance\category-tied_predicate\job\sprout.

the appearance of *la chance* is similar to that of Simone. She goes one step farther when she explicitly focuses on its source:

La chance maybe is to achieve something that you never thought you could achieve. Yeah, that's la chance. You want something, but you're aware that you'll never get it if you don't have la chance. But there is God, who provides you with just some little thing, but this gets things moving so that you'll get it. That's la chance. (Interview 2015 with Simone, 24, law-school graduate; my translation.)[13]

*La chance* is referred to as being beyond what seems to be possible and, simultaneously, as »just some little thing«. It is personal effort plus God rewarding you with *la chance* that finally enables you to move forward.

Once *la chance* has been identified individuals need to ›work with *la chance*‹, which is still part of the process of ›opening up *la chance*‹. ‹Working with *la chance*‹ is characterised by practices of transformation, as I shall now explore.

## Working with *la chance:* Transformation

To begin, it is important to note that working with *la chance* differs significantly from looking for *la chance*. ›Looking for‹ refers to practices that are not directed towards a specific goal but rather an idea (for example, employment). Practices of ›looking for‹ *la chance* result in finding *la chance*. ›Working with‹, on the other hand, is directed towards a specific, anticipated outcome that has been inspired by the sprout of *la chance*. The product of working with *la chance* is the very possession of *la chance*.

In my daily life, well, I'm at work and I work correctly. It's in this sense that I'm provoking ma chance right now. You know, one day when they do their evaluation, they'll say: ›this guy is working well, we should put him in another position‹. So, it is in this sense that I'm provoking ma chance. (Interview 2015 with Oumar, 27, economics graduate; my translation.)[14]

He refers to his job, which he does diligently because he anticipates company evaluations. He mentions nothing concrete but he anticipates

---

13 | Code: la_chance\category-tied_predicate\achievement\sprout.
14 | Code: la_chance\category-bound_activity\opening_up\anticipation\working_with.

other potential positions for him within the company. He is working correctly and thereby provokes *la chance* to be considered for another job. He is preparing. He cannot think of any other action that provokes *la chance*. According to him, *la chance* is something he can provoke by preparing for an anticipated outcome.

By creating serious relationships, I mean: we are collaborating right now and I'm going to be serious about it, and I'm not going to lie to you, I'm going to be honest. If you find something that corresponds to my profile, you won't hesitate to contact me, right? And that's it. (Interview 2015 with Siaka, 29, English graduate; my translation.)[15]

How, then, does Siaka open up *la chance* on his own? He establishes professional relationships by being honest and dutiful. This is his means of establishing himself as a present collaborator and proving himself worthy for possible future collaboration. This is how he makes sure that I think of him in case an opportunity arises for him in the future. He would not only be serious within this relationship, but with everyone around him. You do not want anyone to think or suggest that you are not serious because this affects your opportunities. If I had heard from someone I trust that Siaka was not serious, I would not have employed him. Far more than merely a type of behaviour you need to apply in relationships that appear to be promising in regard to employment opportunities, being serious is a characteristic that is of greater general value because it works beyond established relationships in both positive and negative ways. As Simone once again reflects on her chance to become an intern at the national television network, she says:

La chance was that we studied hard, that we understood our lessons and were thirsty for knowledge. We were worried and we managed to get out and it's also because of us that this chance worked out. (Interview 2015 with Simone, 24, law-school graduate; my translation.)[16]

---

15 | Code: la_chance\category-bound_activity\opening_up\professionality\working_with.

16 | Code: la_chance\category-bound_activity\opening_up\studying\working_with.

I specifically ask her about the saying that I heard from a friend in Mali, which is about God providing *la chance* and man's ability to open it on his or her own as well. She says that it is true, since it is God who provides the opportunities. She was amongst the five best students in her class, and this assured her an internship at a television station. And, she continues, it was due to her studying well and staying on at the station as an unpaid intern that made *la chance* work. She speaks of *la chance* that »a pu fonctionner« – that worked out. Thus, *la chance* is not something that is supposed to work just like that but, instead, it is something people need to work with. *La chance* is presented as an opportunity that has been recognised and exploited as such by, in this case, Simone. Therefore, had she not worked with *la chance* or, to put it differently, not participated in the development of *la chance*, it would not have flourished. The final part of this contribution picks up this notion of flourishing *la chance* and presents the third, and last, type of *la chance*.

## Outcome: Possession

*La chance* transformed is called *sa chance* – her/his chance. As a possession, *la chance* is considered to be the outcome of a completed process of ›opening up *la chance*‹. This exact outcome will then turn into the first type of *la chance* as a requisite in the ongoing process of ›opening up *la chance*‹.

Siaka simply found a job, and he terms this happenstance ›la chance‹. This type of *la chance* is recognised not only by the graduate who finds it but also by the people around him:

We say that someone who's got la chance is someone who's got something. Do you understand what I want to say? If you get something, we say you have la chance. But if you don't have anything, no one is going to say that you have la chance. So, you've got to look for it. That's it. (Interview 2015 with Siaka, 29, English graduate; my translation.)[17]

›Not to have something‹ is not *la chance*. But if you have something, others will observe that. This type of *la chance* is about making *la chance* your own. Siaka said earlier: »You have to look for it and *la chance* will come.«

---

17 | Code: la_chance\category-tied_predicate\possession\outcome.

But *la chance* itself is nothing. »It's about possession, about what we have,« he adds. Hence, if you happen to have *la chance* without looking for it, you would still have to deal with it in order to make it work for you. Once the sprout is identified it flourishes in the process of working with *la chance* until the crop is ready to be harvested.

In summary, there are different states of *la chance*. Residence in a certain area can be *la chance*, but only for those who use it that way, for those who benefit from it. Many people live in the same area but not all of them are considered to have *la chance* – only some have it. *La chance* is not for everyone; rather, it is distinctive. It is recognised in retrospect once it is owned, if it has been grasped or transformed from sprout into possession, from *la chance* to ›sa chance‹ (›her or his chance‹). Others would only recognise *la chance* when it is in the state of possession.

## Conclusion

In this contribution I have introduced the process of ›opening up *la chance*‹ as a way in which Malian graduates manage uncertainty. My initial understanding of *la chance* as a single, ambiguous phenomenon shifted to distinguish between various forms of *la chance* that are distinct in terms of characteristics and practices. Ultimately, three types of *la chance* have been identified: prerequisites, sprouts and outcomes. They are interconnected through practices of ›opening up *la chance*‹ – a process that consists of ›looking for‹, ›finding‹ and ›working with‹ *la chance*. Furthermore, I demonstrate that the phenomenon of *la chance*, as experienced by university graduates, is a process that includes persistent preparation in addition to the identification of a precise moment in time – a sprout of *la chance* – that enables futures.

The aim of this paper has been to disentangle both the various layers and the ambiguity of *la chance*. By applying Membership Categorisation Analysis to sections of my data, I have been able to systematically distinguish between what *la chance* is (category-tied predicates) and which practices are connected with *la chance* (category-bound activities).

In parallel to ethnomethodology's popular example of the logical »the baby cried; the mother picked it up« (Francis and Hester 2004: 47), as opposed to the confusing »The mother cried; the baby picked her up«, the relationship between the graduate and *la chance* is revealed. There is no inherent awkwardness here, which is one of the reasons why *la chance* appears to be ambiguous in the first place. To repeat, »the graduate cried; *la chance* picked her/him up.« (The graduate was preparing. *La chance* appeared.) And vice versa: »*La chance* cried; the graduate picked it up.« (*La chance* appeared. The graduate identified it.) This relationship demands attention in regard to both ends: the graduate demands attention from *la chance* as the graduate enforces it. *La chance* demands the graduate's attention as well, since it needs to be identified and transformed. All in all, Membership Categorisation Analysis has been instrumental in overcoming the first impression that *la chance* is ambiguous by disclosing the interplay between *la chance* and the graduate.

Now that the baby has been picked up, the question is: what happens next? What happens after the baby is picked up by the mother? How does the baby react? Maybe the baby stops crying, maybe the baby even starts to laugh or continues to cry. And what about the mother? Maybe she nurses the baby; maybe she lulls the baby to sleep or hands the baby over to her husband. The point is that the interaction does not end with the mother picking up the baby. Similarly, the process of ›opening up *la chance*‹ does not end with *la chance* being identified by the graduate: *la chance* is further transformed into the graduate's own requisite. And once *la chance* is owned, the graduate will look for further *la chance*.

›Opening up *la chance*‹ means ›seizing promising chances‹ (see Johnson-Hanks 2005), but it is also about identifying and creating ›promising chances‹. The process of ›opening up *la chance*‹ acknowledges university graduates' contribution to the appearance of such ›promising chances‹, which they (and I) call ›la chance‹. Whereas ›judicious opportunism‹ is about working with a sprout of *la chance* only, ›opening up *la chance*‹ begins earlier – with preparation, in particular by generating expertise and by planting seeds. To be prepared means to be attentive: no sprout will go unnoticed or, even worse, get crushed underfoot. It is the process of ›opening up *la chance*‹ that problematises how opportunities are evaluated and adapted to, but also how they are prepared for and created.

›Judicious opportunism‹ argues that »the actor seizes promising chances« (Johnson-Hanks 2005: 363). It is about evaluating and anticipating a ›chance‹ to be ›promising‹, and also about acting accordingly by ›seizing‹ such ›promising chances‹. ›Judicious opportunism‹ requires adaptation, flexibility and evaluation based on »contingent, sudden, and surprising offers that life can make. On the basis of these offers, the aspirations, once vague, will be concretized« (ibid.: 376). In other words, ›judicious opportunism‹ is about reacting in response to an opportunity once it appears (I regard this »offer« as a sprout of *la chance*). It is a strategy characterised by reaction, and it answers the question of how an individual responds to situations of uncertainty, even as it fails to fully recognise the ability of young graduates to create ›promising chances‹ on their own.

In conclusion, university graduates in Bamako create certainty as they open up *la chance*. It is their conviction that *la chance* exists, which is informed by their experiences, in combination with their practices of ›opening up *la chance*‹ (that is, looking for *la chance*, finding *la chance*, and working with *la chance*) that create certainty. University graduates know what they want their futures to look like and what they want to become in the future. Uncertainty about their future does not manifest itself in graduates' daily practices; rather, it circles around the question of when it is that these efforts will flourish. *La chance* delivers the answer because its appearance catalyses the future.

## Bibliography

APEJ (Agence pour la Promotion de l'Emploi des Jeunes). 2011. *Présentation de l'agence pour la promotion de l'emploi des jeunes*. Bamako: APEJ.

Francis, David, Stephen Hester. 2004. *An Invitation to Ethnomethodology: Language, Society and Interaction*. London: Sage.

Johnson-Hanks, Jennifer. 2005. »When the Future Decides: Uncertainty and Intentional Action in Contemporary Cameroon.« *Current Anthropology* 46(3): 363-385.

Silverman, David. 1998. *Harvey Sacks: Social Science and Conversation Analysis*: Oxford: Oxford University Press.

Stokoe, Elizabeth. 2012. »Moving Forward with Membership Categorization Analysis: Methods for Systematic Analysis.« *Discourse Studies* 14 (3): 277-303.

Ten Have, Paul. 2004. *Understanding Qualitative Research and Ethnomethodology*. London: Sage.

© Fatoumata Traoré

© Zoumana Sidibé

© Oumou Traoré

# 5 Looking for Better Opportunities
## An Analysis of Guinean Graduates' Agency

*Carole Ammann*

## INTRODUCTION

Young Guinean graduates' future dreams are quite clear: first, they want to generate a steady and respectable income that enables them and their families to lead a secure and decent life. However, they face prevailing uncertainties that make the fulfilment of this aspiration more and more difficult: as opposed to the period of Guinea's first president Ahmed Sékou Touré between 1958 and 1984, when graduates were guaranteed employment by the state (Camara 2014: 165), gaining a regular salary after their university studies is a major problem today. According to young graduates, their professional objectives are best reached by finding a post in the private sector, especially in one of the well-paying mining companies. Of course they would also welcome employment in the state's administration – not out of prestige or due to the salary, but because it offers social security. Second, in order to be considered as adults and recognised members of their society, young graduates long for marriage and having children. In Kankan, being married and having children is very important for a woman's social status. Hence, women are exposed to much pressure from their families. A male's status, in contrast, is very much interlinked with the image of the family-provider.

Drawing on the life of Djénabou, a 30-year-old woman who holds a Bachelor's degree in political philosophy from the Julius Nyéréré University in Kankan, this contribution closely looks at the agency of young graduates in a Muslim environment.¹ It asks how Djénabou's past habits and the imagination of her future influence the evaluation of her actual situation and thus trigger her everyday practices. How does she seek to seize and hold on to an elusive future? By taking Djénabou's account as its starting point, this contribution more generally traces young graduates' past experiences, as well as their fears, hopes and desires regarding an imagined future. Finally, it analyses the differences between male and female graduates' strategies to tame their uncertainties.²

In recent decades, research on (African) youth has become fashionable in social science. Regarding Guinea there are just a few authors who write about young people, most of whom concentrate on the capital city Conakry. Berliner (2005) looks at youth's religious memories and cultural transmissions, while Philipps and Grovogui (2010) and Philipps (2013) analyse youth involvement in political protests. Straker (2007; 2009) and Engeler (2008; 2015; 2016) both focus on young people and the state in the Forest Region. Finally, Dessertine (2013) examines young people

---

**1** | I do not perceive ›being young‹ as having a certain age but rather in relation to a specific context (Durham 2000). The local definition of youth in Kankan is very flexible. It does not refer to a particular age nor does being married, having children, or having a good job directly mean a person has become an adult. Youth also refers to a person's attitude, for example spending time with young people or being concerned about their preoccupations. One aspect of being young includes having spare time. As women in Kankan have many family obligations – irrespective of whether they are married and have children or not – they are usually considered to be adults much earlier than men are. Additionally, youth as a category is referred to under specific circumstances, for instance to make claims vis-à-vis elders or the state.

**2** | This article is based on ethnographic field research (a total of twelve months between September 2011 and February 2013) for my doctoral thesis. Data gathering focused on the mapping of social actors, discourse and social practice analysis (Förster et al. 2011). Through participation in, observation of, and conversations about the everyday life of sixteen graduates (eleven of whom were male and five female) I approached their present uncertainties and future imaginations. To ensure anonymity I changed all names except in the cases of Thierno and Djénabou, who had asked to be cited by their proper names. I have translated every statement into English myself, and the original (unchanged) French version is in the footnotes.

and mobility in the Upper Guinean Region. However, there is a lack of scholarly work on young Guinean graduates (for an exception, see Engeler 2016).

Drawing upon Emibayer and Mische (1998), the first part of this article looks at iteration, projection and evaluation as the choral triad of agency. In the second part I then recount the life trajectory of Djénabou. On the basis of this example, I discuss in the third part in a more general way the interwoven layers and diversity of young graduates' agency in dealing with uncertainty and shaping their future. I conclude by summarising and discussing the findings.

## Analysing agency

Much of the literature on agency analyses a person's capacity to act individually in a given context, »independently of structural constraints« (Rapport and Overing 2013: 3). Agency »unfolds always through a complex interplay between individual improvisation and the dialogic imagination of a larger whole« (McLean 2007: 7). Anthropologists have criticised agency as being a eurocentric concept because it focuses too much on bargaining (Keane 2003).[3] Mahmood (2005), for example, suggests that we think about agency beyond the notion of resistance. In this context I do not understand agency just as bargaining based within present actions but, following Emirbayer and Mische (1998), in its three temporal dimensions. If we take into account the habitual context, the local social practices and norms, and the imagination of the future we attain a more complete and nuanced understanding of a person's agency. Emirbayer and Mische maintain that the nature of actors' experience is temporal. They see agency as

the temporally constructed engagement by actors of different structural environments – the temporal-relational contexts of action – which, through the interplay of habit, imagination, and judgment, both reproduces and transforms those struc-

---

[3] | I define bargaining as any one of a number of different actions between two or more persons, groups or institutions. Bargaining occurs on a daily basis and does not necessarily contain a mutual, oral agreement – on the contrary, most bargaining processes are nonverbal.

tures in interactive response to the problems posed by changing historical situations (Emirbayer and Mische 1998: 970).

Thus, one's past experiences and habits, one's imagination of what the future may hold, and one's judgment and evaluation of the present are interconnected and constantly influence agency, even though the temporal orientation of specific actions varies.

Through their repetition and continuity, past experiences add to order and stability in an individual's identity and in their agency. Habitual actions are incorporated into thoughts and bodily experiences. In familiar situations such repetitive activities are taken for granted and, thus, are not something of which one is conscious. Through these habitual actions norms and social patterns are produced and reproduced (Emirbayer and Mische 1998: 975-984). Taylor (2002: 106) sees collective practices of group life embedded in the »social imaginary«, which includes normative expectations of how things are and how they ought to be (cf. Castoriadis 1987). Norms of respectability and morality are gendered – in Kankan as well as elsewhere. Norms are imposed through positive and negative sanctions, the enforcement of which provides the individual, group or institution with power (Eriksen 2001 [1995]: 59). However, such morality is not fixed but rather shaped and reshaped through daily interactions, and therefore different conventions and practices co-exist (Olivier de Sardan 2008: 14; Rapport and Overing 2013: 7). As I argue below, habitual local norms have a huge impact on male and, especially, on female graduates' everyday lives.

Life consists of more than habits and routines. Actors constantly imagine their future, which they at times »hope for and try to bring about or fear and seek to avert« (Johnson-Hanks 2002: 872). When unknown and challenging situations arise, past experiences may not help; past responses may not fit (Förster forthcoming: 7). The result is a temporary dislocation that necessitates new, untried actions. These situations prompt the actors to scrutinise habits and past occurrences and to be creative in their search for alternatives;[4] it is at that point that the imagining of possible new patterns is born (Emirbayer and Mische 1998: 983-993). This may result in a conflict between current local norms and the imagination of different possibilities (Rapport and Overing 2013:

---

4 | On agency and creativity, see Förster and Koechlin (2011).

7). However, as the case of Djénabou will illustrate, young graduates do not always challenge the values of their elders. Along with Emirbayer and Mische (1998: 984), I agree that »the formation of projects is always an interactive, culturally embedded process by which social actors negotiate their paths toward the future [...].« Nevertheless, thanks to this ›projective‹ or ›foresightful‹ dimension of agency (Emirbayer and Mische 1998: 983) people expand the horizon of their possible responses. Over the course of time, the imagination and creativity of the individual's responses may have an impact on the larger social environment if social imaginaries change (Taylor 2002).

The unpredictable but imagined future, what Crapanzano (2003: 15) calls ›imaginative horizons‹, also influences the third dimension of agency, namely the present situation, and vice versa. People reflect on, ponder, judge and evaluate possible responses in regard to the demands of specific, conflicting circumstances. Thus, actors constantly deal with ever-shifting settings, a conscious process of daily manoeuvring. In some circumstances they agree with and behave according to habitual practices, while in others they may have to challenge, resist, subvert and contest them. Possible courses of action are evaluated against the background of habits, on the one hand, and of imagined future trajectories, on the other hand (Emirbayer and Mische 1998: 994-1002). To sum up, an individual's agency is not only influenced by contemporary bargaining processes, but also by past experiences and the opening-up of new possibilities in regard to an imagined future.

Another helpful concept for the analysis of young graduates' life situations is the theory of vital conjuncture proposed by Johnson-Hanks (2002). A vital conjuncture is a specific moment in a person's life, referred to as »a socially structured zone of possibilities« (Johnson-Hanks 2002: 871). By looking at this concept through the lenses of agency, vital conjunctures are characterised by habits through »recurring systematicness« and »structured expectations« (ibid.: 872). Imagination, for its part, is present through a high degree of uncertainty and potential transformation, in brief through »contexts of unique possibility and future orientation« (ibid.). One such vital conjuncture occurs when university studies end. This »nexus of potential social futures« (ibid.: 871) can have multiple outcomes: a young female graduate can marry, become a mother, or both, one after the other. Furthermore, she can obtain her first job, change her place of living or even emigrate. However, her husband can also leave her, she can end up unemployed or be obliged to look after her sick parents. Thus, during such special moments full of »uncertainty, promise, or fear« (ibid.: 872) much is at stake because a person's future orientation can change radically.

The following life story shows what everyday practices of a young, female graduate in Kankan look like. I will analyse the impact of iteration and the imagination of an elusive future on the judgment and evaluation of challenging situations. My methodological approach relies on Ahearn (2001), following which I have inquired into the local young graduates' own concepts of agency:

[...] it is important to ask how people themselves conceive of their own actions and whether they attribute responsibility for events to individuals, to fate, to deitles, or to other animate or inanimate forces. (Ahearn 2001: 13)

## Djénabou's life trajectory

Djénabou was born in Kankan in 1986. She is a faithful Muslim who prays several times a day. Djénabou grew up in an area of the city with a bad reputation that is considered as poor by Kankan's inhabitants. She is of Fulani ethnicity and the seventh-oldest out of eleven siblings.[5] Djénabou's father is a retired tailor and the second muezzin of a nearby mosque. Her mother has been engaged in petty trade and presently sells sweets on a table in front of their house. Because of economic hardship, a friendly family raised Djénabou during her school years. Djénabou reiterated how grateful she is that they had encouraged her to study hard at school. As a result, she was always amongst the best in her class, competing with the boys rather than the other girls, as she repeatedly emphasised. Unlike many young women in Kankan – as, for example, her sisters – Djénabou

---

**5 |** The Fulani, numerous and wide-spread throughout West Africa, constitute one of Guinea's four main ethnic groups. In the literature, they are also referred to as Peul or Peuhl (Andrews 2013; Camara et al. 2014: 154). I consider ethnicity to be a fluid category that may change over time and can vary from place to place. Communities typically attribute to themselves shared cultural values and practices, and a shared language. They tend to place great importance on their imagined historical origins (Migdal 2004: 6; Young 2007: 250).

did not leave school after several years to marry but instead earned her diploma and wanted to go to university. Her father, however, was quite sceptical and did not like the idea of one of his daughters pursuing her educational ambitions without first getting married. The fact that all of Djénabou's elder sisters, whose husbands he had chosen for them, had separated eventually made him change his mind; she was thus able to earn a Bachelor's degree in political philosophy. While still a teenager Djénabou became a member of different NGOs.[6] As a result, she gained work experience, met interesting people and visited other parts of the country. Djénabou's father did not like her travelling around and being together with men. Yet he knew that this was an opportunity for his daughter to generate some income, thus contributing to the low family budget.

Equipped with her Bachelor's degree, Djénabou found a job as a teaching assistant at university. Working conditions were not favourable, but it was better than being unemployed – the fate of all too many young graduates. Whenever possible Djénabou took on other job opportunities; she was one of my two research assistants throughout my fieldwork,[7] and she acted as an election observer in her district during the legislative elections of 2013. She supported her family with the money she earned, for example by buying material to construct a washing area. She also paid for a water connection in the compound. Now that running water is available, Djénabou's mother is able to earn some change by letting neighbours pay to refill their tanks. In 2012 Djénabou, her elder brother and a cousin started constructing three boutiques at the nearby roadside. In this regard, Thierno, my other research assistant, admiringly remarked:

What Djénabou does for her family is not self-evident. Usually young women just think of their boyfriends and spend their money in other forms. They buy fancy

---

6 | Usually, these NGOs are not very active in daily life. However, if one of their projects is being financed (such as awareness-raising programmes prior to the presidential elections of 2010) they pursue a range of different activities.

7 | I have elaborated elsewhere on the collaboration with research assistants in ethnographic fieldwork (Ammann, Kaiser-Grolimund and Staudacher 2016).

dresses and shoes to wear for the next wedding or a new cell phone or even a KTM [trendy, Chinese motorcycle]. (Informal conversation 24 February, 2012.)[8]

Whenever we met elderly people, they praised Djénabou for being not only smart but also faithful, respectful and helpful. After teaching at university she usually returned home immediately to cook for everybody. However, Djénabou's university studies, her engagement in the NGOs and, above all, her financial support of the family have not escaped criticism. Some of her elder brothers and sisters do not like the fact that she has succeeded where they have not.

Djénabou is not married yet, but she hopes to find an appropriate husband soon: an intellectual who understands her and will treat her well. He has to be faithful, monogamous and supportive of her decision to engage in various activities. However, Djénabou is keenly aware that finding a husband who matches her imagination will not be easy: »I am one of my family's hopes. If I marry and the marriage fails, my family will suffer,« Djénabou wrote (letter 21 June, 2013).[9] Even though she is not a mother yet, Djénabou assumed this role some years ago when she started caring for her homonym, who is the daughter of a relative.[10] When it comes to men, Djénabou behaves according to local Fulani norms. During the time of research, she was seeing a young man whom she knew from her school days. Djénabou was very careful not to visit his family too often because, she explained, otherwise a future marriage would not be well regarded. Djénabou also emphasised that she remains a virgin. This fact not only makes her parents proud but also increases her attraction as a future wife.

---

8 | »Ce que Djénabou fait pour sa famille, ce n'est pas évident du tout. Normalement les jeunes filles pensent seulement à leur copain et surtout comment acheter des nouvelles robes et souliers pour le prochain mariage. Ou bien elles s'achètent un portable ou même une KTM.«

9 | »Je suis un des espoirs de ma famille, si je me marie et que ça échoue c'est ma famille qui souffrira.«

10 | In Guinea, homonyms are people with the same first name. The relationship between homonyms is often very close. In Kankan it is not uncommon during childhood to spend some time in the family of one's homonym. On reasons for child fosterage in neighbouring Sierra Leone, see Bledsoe (1990).

It is very complicated to be a Fulani. If a young Fulani woman becomes pregnant without being married, she has no value anymore; her father feels like she has dishonoured him and his authority. I don't want this happening to me! (Informal discussion 15 March, 2012.)[11]

Djénabou is afraid that her father will run out of patience and try to marry her to someone she does not like, as he already once before tried to do, in the summer of 2012. The suitor, a close friend of her father's and a distant relative, already had a wife. According to Djénabou he did not treat women respectfully and was very egoistic. Therefore, she refused to marry him.

With the financial help of a cousin, Djénabou could start a Master's degree in human resources at a private university in Conakry in autumn 2013. In the evenings she attended additional classes, for example in computer science. During her free time she was busy writing poems and a novel. At the beginning of her stay in Conakry, Djénabou lived with her aunt, but tense relations in the house became too stressful for her. With the approval of her father she then moved in with the family of a friendly female student. After graduation Djénabou was lucky enough to find temporal employment in a project. Suddenly she acquired the label *directrice du cabinet* (cabinet director) and found herself in a fancy office. She happily wrote: »Thank God I have this contract. My life will change soon« (letter 28 August, 2014).[12] However, Djénabou quit the job after not receiving her salary for two consecutive months. In fact, she is still à la recherche d'opportunités d'emploi (looking for job opportunities) in Conakry. If it does not work out well in the capital city she plans to go back to Kankan, where she would again take up her teaching and NGO activities.

On the one hand, Djénabou has high hopes regarding her future; she dreams of becoming a foreign ambassador someday. On the other hand, she is aware that her chances of ever getting steady employment are quite slim. Nevertheless, she is optimistic: »With my new degree and my

---

**11** | »Chez nous les Peuls, c'est très compliqué. Si tu tombes en grossesse hors mariage, tu n'as plus de valeur. Le père pense que tu as défié son autorité. Je ne veux pas que ça m'arrive!«

**12** | »Dieu merci j'ai eu ce contrat. Ma vie changera bientôt.«

relations, hope is still very big« (letter 25 March, 2014).[13] Djénabou's most urgent problem, however, is not her job situation but her marriage plans:

I think I will marry soon because my whole family dreams just of that. When I come back [from Conakry] there will be much pressure on me. The Master's degree was my excuse, but now, you see... I grow older and now I want to marry. (Letter 15 March, 2014.)[14]

## Between searching for a job and looking for a husband

If I could choose between a job and a husband, I would not know which one to take. (Mariam, young graduate, informal conversation, 6 March, 2012.)[15]

### Dreaming of marriage

Djénabou is still a virgin and belongs to the Fulani. According to Djénabou, the latter aspect complicates her search for a future husband, a man she would like to choose herself, for two reasons: among the Fulani virginity has immense social and economic value, and because marriages within extended families are common (Furth 2005: 237-241; Andrews 2013: 52). Virginity is of huge importance in other ethnic groups as well. However, according to local discursive formations norms are more restrictive within the Fulani, who are said to practice a restrained form of Islam (Gordon 2000: 319; Steady 2011: 64). Marrying and having children is highly important for a woman's respect and place in Guinean society (Doumbouya 2008: 77; Engeler 2015: 103-121).[16] Usually, women marry

---

**13** | »Avk c nvo diplom e mes rlat6n l espoir est encor tres grand.«

**14** | »G pnse m marier osi kr toute la fmille n rev ke d sa e a mn rtour il aura la pression sr moi le master etait mon excuse mais a present tu vois... j'avance en age e j ai envie maintenant d m marier.«

**15** | »Si on me donnait un bon emploie ou un mari à choisir, je ne serais pas quoi prendre...«

**16** | The special issue of *Africa Today* (N.N. 2016) offers more information on ethnographic examples regarding marriage in African countries as well as providing an overview on various issues that have been in the focus of anthropological research.

and have children at an early age. I was told that some young women therefore fear to start university without first marrying.

Although Djénabou is not married yet, she took on the role of a foster mother for her homonym. This decision is clearly future-oriented. In a socially accepted way it enables her to learn how to care for a child and thus become a ›good‹ mother in an imagined future. In general, studying is an accepted excuse to postpone marriage; but as soon as Djénabou finished her Master's degree in summer 2014, the pressure from her family increased. It is still not easy for a young woman in Kankan to choose her future husband; high social and economic pressures prevail (cf. Whitehouse 2016). Thus, the problem is not marriage itself but, instead, the major challenge is to find a worthy husband who will not make her future life too difficult, as Djénabou repeatedly complained. She successfully managed to convince her father that his friend would not be a suitable husband for her. However, Djénabou is unsure whether he would accept her refusal a second time.

An additional problem is that female students and graduates have a bad reputation; gossip about sexual favours or prostitution is omnipresent (cf. Brand 2001; Sommers 2010: 327; Honwana 2012: 91-94). Some men are wary of intellectual women and suspect that they are more likely than illiterate women to oppose the practice of polygamy. And the facts bear out this suspicion: polygamy rates for well-educated and illiterate women are 33 per cent and 56 per cent, respectively (République de Guinée 2006: 97). The last woman a man wishes to marry is one who, knowing that she is his intellectual superior, dares to disobey him. Popular belief has it that such behaviour immediately leads to the cursing of the children and that marriage to such a ›rebel‹ invariably ends in divorce.

Djénabou is aware that polygamy is an integral part of Guinean society. She stressed that she is not opposed to polygamy in principal, as long as the man lives up to his duties as defined in the Qur'an: to feed the whole family and to accord equal treatment to his wives. She complained, however, that in reality this is never the case and that was why she dreaded the prospect of ending up in a polygamous household. How to find an appropriate husband – somebody who would treat her well and support her various activities – was a constant topic of conversation for female graduates like Djénabou. She and her friend Aishatou, who holds a Bachelor's degree in sociology, explained:

A woman who has been to university has a bad reputation. People imagine things. Perhaps this has some truth to it, but it is not always the truth. People say: ›Oh, an educated woman is full of herself. She wants to dominate the household.‹ So not many men want to accept and understand you if you have been to university. If your education achieves a higher level, you are already rejected by a certain part of the society; you are not highly esteemed. (Group discussion 29 January, 2013.)[17]

Marrying and founding a family is also a huge challenge for male graduates. However, for them it is less a question of finding an adequate wife and more of having enough money, first, to pay for the expensive wedding, and second, to settle down. Typically, male graduates dream about constructing their own house where they could take care of their whole family. According to local public opinion men should be the family's primary breadwinners, and this puts much pressure on male graduates. Consequently, in Guinea like in most other West African countries, founding a family has become increasingly difficult for young men and, hence, they marry much later than women (Sommers 2010: 326-327; Honwana 2012: 104; Whitehouse 2016: 33).[18] Sory, a 30-year-old tutor, rhetorically asked: »Now I feel like marrying, but how can I do that...?« (Interview 24 December, 2012.)[19]

## Imagining being a ›good‹ woman

In her article *Bargaining with Patriarchy* Kandiyoti (1988) argues that women strategically bargain different aspects in life to enhance their social security and personal advantages without fundamentally challenging male supremacy. Following this approach, Avishai, Gerber and Randes (2012: 404) write that »women are strategic actors who navigate and appropriate

---

**17** | »Donc aussi une fille qui a été à l'uni est mal vu par la société, les gens se font des imaginations. Peut-être il y a une part de vérité, mais ce n'est pas toujours vérité. On dit: ›Ah, une femme qui a été à l'école est orgueilleuse, intègre, elle veut toujours dominer le foyer.‹ Donc peut d'homme veulent t'accepter et te comprendre si tu as été à l'uni. Si tes études atteignent le niveau supérieur, déjà tu es rejetée d'une certaine manière par la société, tu es mal vu.«

**18** | Whereas in Guinea only 3 per cent of women are still celibate at the age of twenty-five, 44 per cent of men are not yet married at this stage (République de Guinée 2006: 96).

**19** | »Maintenant j'ai envie de me marier, mais comment faire...?«

a complex terrain of domestic, economic, and religious practices and expectations in meeting the demands of contemporary life.« In other words, women, especially well-educated young graduates in Kankan and elsewhere, understand the rules of the game and know how to play it. And sometimes they imagine new or slightly different rules.

Among all the possible futures, becoming a ›good‹ woman is a central identity for most young women in Kankan, regardless of their educational, ethnic or economic backgrounds. Djénabou tries to obtain this attribute by adhering to local social norms: for example, she follows the ritual prayers, neither smokes nor drinks alcohol, and dresses properly.[20] Additionally, Djénabou is respectful towards her parents, elderly relatives and neighbours. Most importantly, however, she does not consort with young men. This behaviour is based on habitual knowledge and is oriented towards an imagined future yet, at the same time, increases her bargaining power in the present. By creating an image of herself as a ›good‹, young Muslim woman, Djénabou hopes to attain several goals: first, elderly family members and neighbours respect her; and second, she has gained her father's confidence. Like this she could travel around for her workshops and to study in Conakry, which is far away from her nuclear family. When Djénabou did not get along with her aunt, her father approved of her moving to a friendly family. Above all, behaving like a ›good‹ young woman enabled her to pursue her academic ambitions and to put off marriage. Because Djénabou always obeyed her father's strictures on dating, she found herself in a good bargaining position when she opposed his choice of a husband; her judgment was respected because her behaviour had been impeccable.

In Kankan women must subordinate themselves to men. From an emic understanding – and in reference to the Qur'an – a woman's (future) children will be cursed if she does not do so. Here, the children metaphorically stand for women's success in the time yet to come. People claim that recent deeds have imminent consequences in an imagined future. Thus, by behaving according to the locally proclaimed gender norms, women may obtain a favourable future. However, if they do

---

**20** | Such dress codes include covering one's legs and not wearing tight trousers. However, different rules exist regarding dressing by day and by night (cf. McGovern 2015: 254).

not conduct themselves accordingly, their future will be under threat.[21] This menace is used as an effective means to enforce the status quo in a patriarchal society. Many men and women, among them Djénabou, see this as an explanation for gender hierarchy in Kankan.

Djénabou subordinates herself to her father, brothers and other men. She does not usually call this habitual practice into question. However, being a young intellectual woman in a place like Kankan, where a strict understanding of gender norms prevails, is not always easy. There are instances when Djénabou, like other female graduates, challenges the habit of female subordination. Djénabou and her friend Aishatou once lamented:

It is true: a woman must submit to her husband. I think this is the case in every community. But here, it is not just that; here, it has a slavish aspect. Women are not allowed to say what they think, they are never right. Everything men do is good, everything women do is bad. And when we went to school we started looking at the world differently. It is hard for us to accept this perception. (Group discussion 29 January, 2013.)[22]

Djénabou and Aishatou state that because of their educational background and NGO activities they are aware of certain forms of gender-related injustice. Their harsh critique must be seen in the context of the difficult social and economic reality that women in Kankan face. On the one hand, they are to behave according to social norms and subordinate themselves to men; on the other hand, they have to gain sufficient resources to sustain their families at times when their husbands

---

**21** | This is also described by Osborn (2011: 28): »Epics, oral traditions, and family histories throughout Mande are sprinkled with women whose humility, courage, sacrifice, and loyalty generate a ›maternal inheritance‹ that enables their children, and especially their sons, to perform great deeds.«

**22** | »C'est vrai, il faut que la femme soit soumise à son mari, je pense que ça existe dans toutes les communautés. Mais ici, c'est pas seulement ça, il y a un côté esclavagiste dedans. La femme n'a pas droit à la parole, elle n'a pas raison, elle ne doit pas discuter. Tout ce que l'homme fait est bon et tout ce que la femme fait est mauvaise. Et quand on a été à l'école on a compris la vie d'une autre manière. C'est difficile d'accepter cette conception pour nous.« Kaufmann (2016) made similar observations in Liberia.

or fathers are not capable of doing so. Nevertheless, men remain the heads of the household.

Djénabou is a Muslim. By and large, religion is very present in the lives of Guinea's population, for the young and the elderly, intellectuals and illiterates alike. Religion as a basic principle penetrates all spheres of people's lives, and it shapes their daily experiences (Smid 2010: 49). Islam is an integral and stabilising element in Djénabou's identity. She respects local Muslim principles and does not question her family's religious practices. Her future husband must be religious too, Djénabou emphasised several times. She refers to God when talking about her future plans. According to Djénabou's explanations, He watches her closely. If she is a ›good‹ woman in the present, this will influence her future in a positive way.

Behaving according to local social norms is also important for male graduates. Similar to Djénabou, they refer to God when elaborating on their dreams. Mamy, who was born in 1984, holds a Master's degree in sociology and works as a tutor at university. While speaking about his academic ambitious, he explained:

I set an objective, but I am also a Muslim, I believe in destiny, in God. […] God knows how much I learned at school, God knows that I am responsible with my parents and my surroundings. He knows that the little I earn I give to my parents. And this same God said that if a child is looking for the blessing of his parents, He would give this child what it requests. So I believe God will give this to me. In regard to academia I also believe in my future. […] I want to continue my studies. In three years' time I want to have my PhD, if God gives me good health and the financial means. […] I will not obtain it [my PhD] easily, while sleeping. I must fight. (Interview 5 February, 2013.)[23]

---

**23** | »Je fixe un objectif, mais aussi, je suis musulman, je crois au destin, en Dieu. […] Dieu sait que je me suis battu à l'école, Dieu sait que je suis sérieux avec mes parents et mon entourage. Il sait que le peu que je gagne, je le mets à la disposition de mes parents. Et ce même Dieu a dit quand un enfant cherche la bénédiction auprès de ses parents il va donner à cet enfant ce qu'il demande. Donc je crois que Dieu va me donner ça. Mais sur le plan scientifique je crois aussi à mon avenir. […] je cherche à continuer mes études. Dans trois ans, je veux avoir

For Mamy, only God knows what his future may hold; He is the one who predestines life. This however does not result in passiveness. On the contrary, by behaving according to local Muslim principles Mamy actively tries to influence his future: he is respectful to elders and sends money to his parents in the village whenever he can. Furthermore, Mamy works hard and takes his studies seriously. As a consequence he receives the blessing from his parents. Due to this blessing, God will help Mamy to achieve his goals. Like other young graduates, Mamy actively participates in his divine destiny and thereby assumes responsibility over his life.

## Improving one's chances by studying

Generally, not many young women in Guinea can study.[24] Female students must cook and do other domestic work and thus cannot invest much time in learning and other activities. Typically, they are strongly guarded and their behaviour is more critically observed than that of their male counterparts.

Guinean graduates regard their university studies as a privilege. At the same time, their academic background implies specific expectations for their future life trajectories. For Djénabou education has always been the key to success, thanks largely to the fact that her homonym's family encouraged her to work hard at school. Djénabou's imaginative horizon features a vision of herself as a caring mother who, at the same time, pursues her professional goals, a supportive, religious husband by her side. Aware that for this vision to become reality she had to acquire further

---

mon doctorat, si Dieu me donne la santé et les moyens [...]. Je n'aurais pas facilement [mon doctorat], pas en dormant, il faut me battre.«

**24 |** The difference between the high number of men and the low number of women at university level is striking (République de Guinée 2006: 37-38). However, this is not a Guinean particularity but a matter of fact throughout Africa; only six per cent of professors at African universities are women (Mama 2007: 4; cf. Okeke-Ihejirika 2009). Writing about Cameroon, Johnson-Hanks remarks that girls who can complete high school »have been unusually successful and their modes of action effective« (Johnson-Hanks 2005: 367), especially insofar as it is much more difficult for girls than for boys to mobilise the necessary financial means to attend school.

professional qualifications, she decided to continue her academic studies in Conakry.

Once they hold a Bachelor's degree young graduates' studies do not come to an end. Knowing that the job market is tough, male as well as female graduates see further education as a key to fulfil their future dreams. English and computer science are the most popular courses offered by private evening schools or workshops on weekends; and it is with such qualifications that young graduates hope to have a better chance on the job market. Similar to Djénabou, many Guinean graduates dream about continuing their academic career. They wish to go abroad on a scholarship, to a place where the educational system is better than in Guinea. In their imagination, they would expand their scientific knowledge and get to know other ways of life; once they return to their country, they would have earned the esteem of their community and improved their chances of finding long-term employment. This imagination is influenced by the life trajectories of important Guinean politicians, such as Alpha Condé, Guinea's president since 2010, who studied political science and holds a PhD in public law from the French university of Sorbonne (Camara et al. 2014: 91).[25] My male interlocutors in particular have the ambition of playing a decisive role in the future of their country. Mamy stated:

> Some of my students call me the future president of the Republic because I have a project, a goal. [...] I tell myself I must serve my country. If in the future someone calls upon the leaders of Guinea, it will be necessary to call upon Mamy Konaté. [...] It is in my dreams: I want to become one of tomorrow's indispensable cadres of this country, and I want to sit at the table to discuss the problems. (Interview 5 February, 2013.)[26]

Personal connections are crucial to access the labour market. For this reason young graduates actively shape their networks: after graduation

---

25 | Kaufmann (2016: 172-176) also describes studying as a strategy for social mobility in the context of post-war Liberia.

26 | »Certains de mes étudiants m'appellent futur président de la république parce que j'ai un projet, un objective. [...] Je me dis je dois servir la Guinée. Quand on va appeler la maison de la Guinée, il faut qu'on appelle Mamy Konaté. [...] C'est dans mes rêves, je veux être un cadre incontournable de ce pays de demain, je sois à la table pour discuter des problèmes.«

new contacts are made, old ones are intensified and others fade or disappear. By continuing their studies young graduates can integrate into new social networks, which may prove helpful one day.

**Looking for opportunities**

Even though Mamy's future dreams of first gaining a PhD and then becoming an important Guinean leader are quite explicit, he is well aware of the country's difficult economic, political and social situation. Therefore he, Djénabou and other graduates always try to pursue the most promising path that could help them one day to achieve their goals. Johnson-Hanks (2005) uses the term »judicious opportunism« to describe this constant evaluation of the present under circumstances in which uncertainty prevails. She states: »The challenge is not to formulate a plan and implement it regardless of what comes but to adapt to the moment, to be calm and supple, recognizing the difference between a promising and an unpromising offer« (Johnson-Hanks 2005: 370).

This continual search for new work opportunities is also present in Djénabou's accounts. After she graduated from university she feared that she would be unemployed, just like most of her peers. When her professor offered her a position as a teaching assistant at university, she accepted despite the bad work conditions there. Djénabou supplemented her small income whenever possible with other temporary jobs, for example, for one of the various NGOs of which she was a member. Elections, as such, create possibilities to get hold of a short-term job. Djénabou acted as an election observer, and Sory was an operator for voter registration. Most of my informants support one of the three significant political parties in Kankan, and they helped in election campaigns for the presidential elections of 2010 and the parliamentary elections of 2013. Djénabou, however, has deliberately never joined a political party because, as she told me, she wanted to remain neutral to keep her image as a bridge-builder and be able to do her different jobs in the NGOs (informal conversation 28 November, 2012).

In general, women's income is seen as suplementary, and men remain the primary breadwinners. The fact that Djénabou contributes substantially to her family's income has earned her entourage's respect. Therefore, the tight family budgets and the general financial uncertainties generate space for Djénabou to manoeuvre as well as providing her with a certain amount of power: she successfully convinced her parents that they would one day benefit from her qualifications. This was why Djénabou's father had to accept her attendance at workshops outside of Kankan. Although he generally disapproves of her travelling around and, thus, associating with men, he acknowledges her occasional income.

One day I was sitting in a café near the university and listened to a fierce discussion between two male students over the kind of employment that was suitable for a graduate. One student claimed that graduates should not accept a job, such as teaching in a primary school, that was not appropriate for them due to their educational background. »You have to choose at your level. Someone who wants a motorcycle does not want a bike,« he argued.[27] The other student disagreed. He said that he would accept any job offered to him, even cleaning the streets, as long as he earned something. »If you are poor, you have no choice,« he stressed (field notes 1 March, 2012).[28] The example shows that it is not only the salary but also a job's reputation that is of importance when evaluating the advantages and disadvantages of a certain job. This could be the reason why young graduates usually do not talk openly about their income-generating activities.

Throughout the day male young graduates, just like non-graduates, are busy with all kind of different things. Such ›hustling‹ (Kaufmann 2016: 166-172) is not easy to understand for an outsider. Some of Kankan's male graduates have started their own small commercial enterprise with the help of so-called big people.[29] Amadou for example now owns two video shops; Saa organised transports between his hometown Guéckédou and Conakry for a period of time; Labila temporarily sold spices on the market and drove a motorbike taxi; and Ismael still earns money by ›traditionally‹ pressing cloths.[30] In Fioratta's (2015: 304) terms, such male youth is »constantly on the lookout for entrepreneurial opportunities«. However,

---

27 | »Il faut décider à la hauteur. Qui veut une moto ne veut pas un vélo.«
28 | »Le fils d'un pauvre n'a pas le choix.«
29 | On the concept of Big Men, see Utas (2012).
30 | In regard to young people in the Fouta Djallon, Fioratta (2015: 302-303) writes: »To show their families and communities that they were, or were becoming, responsible adult persons, both men and women occupied themselves with entrepreneurial ventures that counted as respectable work, even when their efforts yielded little or no profit.«

none of my female informants started their own businesses, although some do help their mothers or relatives to sell items on the market or in a boutique. As opposed to male graduates, female graduates usually do not hustle, and they must reveal exactly where they are going and why everytime they leave home.

Some graduates teach courses at private secondary schools, and others, like Djénabou, work as tutors at university once they have completed their Bachelor's degree. This is a way of earning a low yet steady income and having the prospect of becoming a state employee. Officially, tutorship is a recruiting system for young graduates with the goal to include them into university staff. However, several tutors stay in that position for years and never become civil servants. Because of their unsatisfactory position, Guinean tutors decided to go on strike at the beginning of 2013 despite the fear of negative personal consequences.

Volunteering in the public or private sector is a way of gaining work experience and enlarging one's networks in order to get a steady job in the future.[31] Being a member of an NGO is another common strategy to establish new personal connections, generate an irregular income, and take part in workshops and training programs to improve one's qualifications. Both of these activities are regarded as a stepping-stone to future employment opportunities and, in some cases, they indeed prove to be.

The constant search for alternatives or secondary employment(s) is also described by Bierschenk (2014: 240) in the case of state employees in Benin, who did not have any particular future career in mind when they entered state service but instead applied for a range of jobs. However, in Bierschenk's words they have only »limited investment in what they are actually doing, and are permanently on the outlook for exit options« (ibid.). This is similar for all graduates in Kankan to whom I have spoken. All of their activities mentioned above are seen as temporal, as a possibility of making a living while waiting for better opportunities. They can be analysed as practices to get a hold on an elusive future. Thus, Johnson-Hanks is correct in claiming that »[m]aintaining options is the central aim of action under judicious opportunism« (Johnson-Hanks 2005: 370).

---

**31** | Blundo and Olivier de Sardan (2006: 78) deal with unpaid jobs in African administrations.

## Discussion

Between order and chaos, between continuity and change, between harmony and conflict lies uncertainty. [...] Uncertainty and insecurity are notions that link the present with the past and the future (Benda-Beckmann and Benda-Beckman 2000: 7).

Young former students evaluate their current situation by recalling past personal experiences and imagining possible future trajectories. The interactions between the three temporal dimensions of agency are evident in Djénabou's narrations. Her habitual religious practices, for example, have a stabilising effect on her identity. The validity of local customs, which from an emic perspective have been transmitted over generations, tends to be taken for granted. Generally, the importance of behaving properly is very much embodied in young graduates' attitudes and habitual actions: You must respect your parents and elders; women must defer to the men in their lives or otherwise their (future) offspring will be cursed. However, as Schroven rightly notes, »there is room for change within the performance of habitual rituals or the possibility to express resistance camouflaged by approval« (Schroven 2010: iii, my translation). It is by imagining potential future trajectories that these graduates create strategies to change their prospects.

Djénabou has various ideas of what she wants in her personal life. She has adopted manifold ways of daily manoeuvring to achieve her goals within the context of Kankan's patriarchal political, social and economic structures. Djénabou's past experience tells her that financial independence is a good tool at her disposal to improve her situation in an imagined future. This knowledge, and her eagerness to learn, influenced her choice of going to university in the first place and then leaving the family to continue her studies in Conakry. Djénabou attributes her present status largely to the fact that she grew up in her homonym's family. But she also accredits the fact that her father accepted her various choices to her behaviour according to local norms. At the same time, Djénabou likes to consider herself a rebel at heart who questions and, sometimes, challenges local norms; but the fact that she won from her father the right to attend university and to refuse marriage to a man who did not suit her derives only from her subordinating her will to his in other domains. Therefore, Djénabou performs a balancing act between, on the one hand, behaving like a ›good‹ Fulani woman and, on the other hand, following her academic ambitions and pursuing her goal to lead an independent life even as a soon-to-be wife.

For young people the end of university studies marks an important stage in their lives. Graduates hope to find a secure job, for example in state administration or in the private sector, preferably in one of the mining or communication companies. Beyond this, they strive to marry and have children. Graduation is not a rupture with the past. Instead, it can be seen as a vital conjuncture marked by a high degree of uncertainty but also future opportunities and transformations (Johnson-Hanks 2002). Uncertainty over future trajectories does not prevent my interlocutors from formulating concrete ambitions. However, even though Djénabou dreams of being a foreign ambassador and Mamy dreams of completing a PhD and becoming one of Guinea's leaders, it is important to note that these are not fixed goals in accordance to which they plan their careers step by step. When talking about their future in the uncertain environment of Guinea, both choose instead to mention various possibilities depending on the available opportunities (cf. Johnson-Hanks 2005: 368).

The personal and professional aspirations of young male and female Guinean graduates, like those of educated Beti women in Cameroon, »are multiple, changeable, and apply over a variety of temporal frames« (Johnson-Hanks 2002: 867). Regarding their imagined future life trajectories, young graduates are torn between hopes and disillusionment evoked by daily realities. As there are almost no possibilities to find fixed employment, they must simultaneously apply different livelihood strategies »while waiting« and looking for better opportunities. The notion of »waithood« (Honwana 2012) is prominent in many conversations with young graduates in Kankan over their job situations. However, their daily practices reveal that they are not just waiting and doing nothing – on the contrary. To echo Honwana's observations: »They identify, explore, and try to maximize whatever opportunities they find in a constant effort to improve their daily lives« (Honwana 2012: 61). Hence, their action is based on ›judicious opportunism‹ (Johnson-Hanks 2005: 363). Sory put it like this:

I am evaluating the matters. In case I have a good chance elsewhere, I can also profit from that. But while waiting, I am here. We are looking for the place where living conditions are best. (Interview 24 December, 2012.)[32]

Young graduates launch various economic activities, accept precarious temporal employment as tutors, teach at secondary schools, gain work experience in unpaid internships, and continue their studies. However, these activities often do not satisfy young graduates' career expectations. At the same time, the different income-generating strategies help to enlarge their networks and open up new possibilities. A Guinean saying goes that the number of individuals you know equals the chances you have.

Marrying and founding a family is an important objective for Guinean graduates which enables them to occupy a respected place in society. Regarding marriage, there is a major difference between male and female graduates: men have far more time at their disposal until they come under social pressure to wed. Thus, they can primarily concentrate on establishing themselves in order to dispose of enough money to finance a pompous marriage, which is quite important for young urban women these days. In this context female graduates again must be active in two domains: first, in the search for job opportunities and, second by looking for a ›good‹ husband. While a man can wait until he is around forty years of age, a woman who is not yet married by the age of twenty-five is in a dire situation. Although it would not be too difficult for female graduates to find a husband, they typically do not imagine their future as only staying at home, taking care of the household, and caring for their husbands. On the contrary, female graduates are ambitious and therefore invest much time and energy into finding a future spouse who fits their imagination: female former students typically look for a man who provides them with sufficient liberties to pursue their own professional ambitions and who fundamentally encourages all of their various activities.[33] Hence, in regard

---

32 | »Je suis aussi en train de voir les choses, au cas où j'aurais une forte chance ailleurs, je peux aussi profiter de cela, mais en attendant je suis là. Nous cherchons là où les conditions de vie son meilleurs.«

33 | Whitehouse (2016) shows the gap between the imagined, idealised future husband and the lived realities of young people in Mali. My data illustrate that this is similar in Kankan.

to marriage young female graduates form a specific category within Kankan's society and are not representative of young women in general.

By looking at young graduates' agency we see that many of their actions are oriented towards an unknown future. The daily realities of Guinean graduates are complex and ever-changing. For precisely the reason that the achievement of their future dreams seems to be so elusive, they apply various strategies to reach their goals. As Johnson-Hanks (2005: 363) rightly notes, we cannot analyse their actions in a causal way: »[...] under the conditions of uncertainty applicable in contemporary Africa, effective social action is based not on the fulfilment of prior intentions but on a judicious opportunism: the actor seizes promising chances.« It goes without saying that the permanent search for opportunities is not limited to graduates but applies to other young men and women in Guinea, too. Every decision they make to tame their unknown future creates new forms of insecurity. However, the educational background of former students does change their ambitions, their possibilities and their strategies of dealing with uncertainty. Djénabou's case is unique because she went to university even though she comes from an underprivileged background where local Muslim and Fulani norms are of huge importance and in which her parents and sisters have at best only basic, formal education.

In a context such as Guinea, which is marked by political, social and economic insecurity, nobody knows which action will finally lead to the realisation of one's ambitions. I argue, therefore, that we must investigate the interwoven layers and diversity of young graduates' agency in order to understand how they try to shape their future life trajectories. A typical pattern here is the flexibility of their actions and the multiplicity in trying to reach their goals. Furthermore, they have faith in God, who chooses what is right for someone. By behaving according to local Muslim principles Guinean graduates desire their parents' blessings. Thus, young graduates actively participate in their divine destiny: because they please God, He will help them to attain their ambitions in a future yet to come.

## Bibliography

Ahearn, Laura M. 2001. »Language and Agency.« *Annual Revue of Anthropology* 30: 109-137.

Ammann, Carole, Andrea Kaiser-Grolimund, Sandra Staudacher. 2016. »Research Assistants. Invisible but Indispensable in Ethnographic Research.« *Tsantsa* 21: 152-156.

Andrews, B. Lacey. N.N. »Family Relations: Sub-Saharan Africa: Fulbe Societies.« in *Encyclopedia of Women & Islamic Cultures* (Brill Online). Retrieved 27 April, 2016. [http://referenceworks.brillonline.com/entries/encyclopedia-of-women-and-islamic-cultures/family-relations-sub-saharan-africa-fulbe-societies-EWICCOM_0077d]

Avishai, Orit, Lynne Gerber, Jennifer Randles. 2012. »The Feminist Ethnographer's Dilemma. Reconciling Progressive Research Agendas with Fieldwork Realities.« *Journal of Contemporary Ethnography* 42(4): 394-426.

Benda-Beckmann, Franz, Keebet Benda-Beckmann. 2000. »Coping with Insecurity.« In *Coping with Insecurity. An ›Underall‹ Perspective on Social Security in the Third World*, edited by Franz Benda-Beckmann, Keebet Benda-Beckmann, Hans Marks. Yogyakarta: Pustaka Pelajar. 7-31.

Berliner, David. 2005. »An ›Impossible‹ Transmission. Youth Religious Memories in Guinea-Conakry.« *American Ethnologist* 32(4): 576-592.

Bierschenk, Thomas. 2014. »Sedimentation, Fragmentation and Normative Double-Binds in (West) African Public Services.« In *States at Work*, edited by Thomas Bierschenk, Jean-Pierre Olivier de Sardan. Leiden and Boston: Brill. 221-245

Bledsoe, Caroline. 1990. »›No Success Without Struggle.‹ Social Mobility and Hardship for Foster Children in Sierra Leone.« *Man* 25(1): 70-88.

Blundo, Giorgio, Jean-Pierre Olivier de Sardan. 2006. *Everyday Corruption and the State. Citizens & Public Officials in Africa*. Cape Town: Zed Books.

Brand, Saskia. 2001. *Mediating Means and Fate. A Socio-Political Analysis of Fertility and Demographic Change in Bamako, Mali*. Leiden and Boston: Brill Academic Pub.

Camara, Mohamed Saliou. 2014. *Political History of Guinea since World War Two*. New York: Peter Lang.

Camara, Mohamed Saliou, Thomas O'Toole, Janice E. Baker. 2014. *Historical Dictionary of Guinea*. Lanham: Scarecrow Press.

Castoriadis, Cornelius. 1987. *The Imaginary Institution of Society*. Cambridge: Polity Press.

Crapanzano, Vincent. 2003. *Imaginative Horizons. An Essay in Literary-Philosophical Anthropology*. Chicago: University of Chicago Press.

Dessertine, Anna. 2013. »Le lu ne meurt jamais. Mobilités des individus et pérennité de la résidence dans un village malinké de Guinée.« *Géocarrefour* 88(2): 131-138.

Doumbouya, Oumar Sivory. 2008. *La situation sociale des femmes en Guinée. De la période précoloniale jusqu'à nos jours*. Paris: L'Harmattan.

Durham, Deborah. 2000. »Youth and the Social Imagination in Africa. Introduction to Parts 1 and 2.« *Anthropological Quarterly* 73(3): 113-120.

Emirbayer, Mustafa, Anne Mische. 1998. »What Is Agency?« *American Journal of Sociology* 103(4): 962-1023.

Engeler, Michelle. 2008. »Guinea in 2008: The Unfinished Revolution.« *Politique Africaine* 112: 87-98.

Engeler, Michelle. 2015. »At the Crossroads. Being Young and the State in the Making in Guéckédou, Guinea.« PhD dissertation, University of Basel.

Engeler, Michelle. 2016. »Being Young in the *Guinée Forestière*: Members of Youth Associations as Political Entrepreneurs.« *Stichproben* 30: 63-86.

Eriksen, Thomas Hylland. 2001 [1995]. *Small Places, Large Issues. An Introduction to Special and Cultural Anthropology*. London: Pluto.

Fioratta, Susanna. 2015. »Beyond Remittance. Evading Uselessness and Seeking Personhood in Fouta Djallon, Guinea.« *American Ethnologist* 42(2): 295-308.

Förster, Till et al. 2011. »The Emic Evaluation Approach – Epistemologies, Experience, and Ethnographic Practice.« *Basel Papers on Political Transformations* 3.

Förster, Till, Lucy Koechlin. 2011. »The Politics of Governance. Power and Agency in the Formation of Political Order in Africa.« *Basel Papers on Political Transformations* 1.

Förster, Till. (Forthcoming.) »Handlungsfähigkeit, Artikulation, Diskurs. Was leistet die politische Anthropologie?« *Praxistheorien in der Ethnologie*.

Furth, Rebecca Courtney. 2005. »Marrying the Forbidden Other. Marriage, Status and Social Change in the Futa Jallon Highlands of Guinea.« PhD dissertation, University of Wisconsin.

Gordon, Andrew J. 2000. »Cultural Identity and Illness. Fulani Views.« *Culture, Medicine and Psychiatry* 24(3): 297-330.

Honwana, Alcinda Manuel. 2012. *The Time of Youth. Work, Social Change, and Politics in Africa.* Sterling: Kumarian Press.

Johnson-Hanks, Jennifer. 2002. »On the Limits of Life Stages in Ethnography. Toward a Theory of Vital Conjunctures.« *American Anthropologist* 104(3): 865-880.

Johnson-Hanks, Jennifer. 2005. »When the Future Decides.« *Current Anthropology* 46(3): 363-385.

Kandiyoti, Deniz. 1988. »Bargaining With Patriarchy.« *Gender & Society* 2(3): 274-290.

Kaufmann, Andrea A. 2016. »Spaces of Imagination. Associational Life and the State in Post-War, Urban Liberia.« PhD dissertation, University of Basel.

Keane, Webb. 2003. »Self-Interpretation, Agency, and the Objects of Anthropology. Reflections on a Genealogy.« *Comparative Studies in Society and History* 45(2): 222-248.

Mahmood, Saba. 2005. *Politics of Piety. The Islamic Revival and the Feminist Subject.* Princeton: Princeton University Press.

Mama, Amina. 2007. »Is it Ethical to Study Africa? Preliminary Thoughts on Scholarship and Freedom.« *African Studies Review* 50(1): 1-26.

McGovern, Mike. 2015. »Liberty and Moral Ambivalence. Postsocialist Transitions, Refugee Hosting, and Bodily Comportment in the Republic of Guinea.« *American Ethnologist* 42(2): 247-261.

McLean, Stuart. 2007. »Introduction. Why Imagination.« *Irish Journal of Anthropology* 10(2): 5-9.

Migdal, Joel S. 2004. »Mental Maps and Virtual Checkpoints. Struggles to Construct and Maintain State and Social Boundaries.« In *Boundaries and Belonging. States and Societies in the Struggle to Shape Identities and Local Practices,* edited by Joel S. Migdal. Cambridge: Cambridge University Press. 3-23.

N.N. 2016. »Special Issue. Objects, Money, and Meaning in Contemporary African Marriage.« *Africa Today* 62(3).

Olivier de Sardan, Jean-Pierre. 2008. »Researching the Practical Norms of Real Governance in Africa.« *Discussion Paper* 5. London: Overseas Development Institute.

Okeke-Ihejirika, Philomina. 2009. »Gender Equity in African Tertiary Education Systems.« In *Power, Gender and Social Change in Africa*, edited by Muna Ndulo and Grieco Margaret. Newcastle: Cambridge Scholars Publishing. 207-229.

Osborn, Emily Lynn. 2011. *Our New Husbands are here. Households, Gender, and Politics in a West African State from the Slave Trade to Colonial Rule.* Athens: Ohio University Press.

Philipps, Joschka. 2013. *Ambivalent Rage. Youth Gangs and Urban Protest in Conakry, Guinea.* Paris: Harmattan.

Philipps, Joschka, Thomas Grovogui. 2015. »Urban Youth and Political Violence in Conakry.« *Baseline Paper* (2010). Retrieved 8 August, 2015. [https://www.sfcg.org/wp-content/uploads/2014/08/GUI_BL_Apr10_Baseline-Paper-Urban-Youth-and-Political-Violence.pdf]

Rapport, Nigel, Joanna Overing. 2013. *Social and Cultural Anthropology. The Key Concepts.* London: Routledge.

République de Guinée. 2006. *Enquête démographique et de santé, Guinée 2005.* Conakry and Calverton: Direction Nationale de la Statistique (DNS) du Ministère du Plan.

Schroven, Anita. 2010. »Integration through Marginality. Local Politics and Oral Tradition in Guinea.« PhD dissertation, Martin-Luther University.

Smid, Karen. 2010. »Resting at Creation and Afterlife. Distant Times in the Ordinary Strategies of Muslim Women in the Rural Fouta Djallon, Guinea.« *American Ethnologist* 37(1): 36-52.

Sommers, Marc. 2010. »Urban Youth in Africa.« *Environment and Urbanization* 22(2): 317-332.

Steady, Filomina Chioma. 2011. *Women and Leadership in West Africa.* New York: Palgrave Macmillan.

Straker, Jay. 2007. »Youth, Globalisation and Millennial Reflection in a Guinean Forest Town.« *Journal of Modern African Studies* 45(2): 299-319.

Straker, Jay. 2009. *Youth, Nationalism, and the Guinean Revolution.* Bloomington: Indiana University Press.

Taylor, Charles. 2002. »Modern Social Imaginaries.« *Public Culture* 14(1): 91-124.

Utas, Mats. 2012. »Introduction. Bigmanity and Network Governance in African Conflicts.« In *African Conflicts and Informal Power. Big Men and Networks*, edited by Mats Utas. London and New York: Zed Books. 1-34.

Whitehouse, Bruce. 2016. »Sadio's Choice. Love, Materialism, and Consensual Marriage in Bamako, Mali.« *Africa Today* 62(3): 28-46.

Young, Crawford. 2007. »Nation, Ethnicity and Citizenship. Dilemmas of Democracy and Civil Order in Africa.« In *Making Nations, Creating Strangers. States and Citizenship in Africa*, edited by Sara R. Dorman et al. Leiden: Brill. 241-264.

# 6 Politics of the Future – Riots of the Now
Temporal Horizons of Youth in Upheavals in England and Guinea

*Joschka Philipps*

## INTRODUCTION

A great deal of politics seems to be about the future, and much of the future seems to be managed by politics. Political networks develop narratives and ordering mechanisms that negotiate continuity and change in societies, and attempt to manage the contingency created by an entirely elusive future. In functionally differentiated societies, Luhmann (2002: 151) suggests that the political system creates the impression of a future that is being taken care of. And in many former colonies, governments find themselves confronted with widespread and long-standing expectations of ›development‹, which are placed in the more or less proximate future (see Mitchell 2014: 500).[1] When studying as to why and how the future is significant for people, it thus becomes important to take a closer look at politics. It should be particularly revealing to look at political upheavals, the »realm of contingency« where the taken-for-grantedness of political regimes is dismantled (Branch and Mampilly 2015: 10), and where uncertainty looms large as to who will deal with the future *in* the future.

In this chapter, I analyse interviews and conversations with young men who were directly involved in popular upheavals in England and Guinea. My central question is how these young men talk about the

---

**1** | Mitchell (2014: 507) delineates how »the future entered government« as a fundamental historical shift in modern political practice after the Second World War in the United States, and argues that politics became »a mode of government-through-the-future.«

political future. While they actively destabilised the present political order, did they see their agency as potentially contributing to a different future? Or did they consider their actions to be short-lived and with no further political impact? I suggest that exploring these questions can tell us a lot about how different political systems, insofar as they include and exclude their citizens in different ways, shape young people's perspectives on the collective future. During my fieldwork in Guinea (2009-2012), where I had studied the involvement of youth gangs in urban protests (Philipps 2011; 2013a; 2013b), I never explicitly asked these questions. Nevertheless, informants and interviewees generally expressed an intense longing for radical political change in the imminent future. The comparison with the English riots of 2011 is born out of a growing curiosity in transcontinental comparative research (see Philipps 2014: 10-11; Robinson 2011), which treats African cases as examples for global dynamics and developments (see e.g. Comaroff and Comaroff 2012a, 2012b; Mbembe and Nuttall 2004; Utas 2014). Looking through the available data on English rioters' perceptions of the future, however, the Guinean and the English case stand in an unexpectedly stark contrast to each other. In a nutshell, while most Guinean young men I talked to between 2009 and 2012 embraced the notion of imminent political change, the English youth I read about seemed to have rioted with no obvious concern for the future at all. This chapter asks how we can make sense of that contrast.

Niklas Luhmann's thoughts about the relation between politics and the future, as well as on trust and confidence, provide a loose collection of ideas to be critically explored in this paper. Luhmann is concerned with the future's uncertainty as an indispensable resource for politics (Luhmann 2002: 147). Broadly, politicians project futures to obtain popular support – they project a bright future provided that they will win the elections, for instance, and a troubling future in case they do not; and any political decision for the future is valorised as »a difference to what would happen if one were to let things simply slide« (Luhmann 2002: 146).[2] As the political system juggles with different futures, usually on a spectrum between utopian and dystopian, and as it makes collectively binding decisions that affect the future, Luhmann (2002: 169) claims that:

---

**2** | My translation from German: »eine Differenz zu dem, was sich ergeben würde, wenn man die Dinge laufen ließe, wie sie nun einmal laufen.«

> The possibility of observing politics [provides] a substitute for the obstructed possibility of observing the future. The future's unknown character, its unobservability is therefore the condition for politics' high level of attention. Not least, this could explain why the observation of politics oscillates between trust and distrust. [...] Politics [functions], so to speak, as the governor [*statthalter*] of the covert, unintelligible future.³

According to Luhmann, the public's observation of politics as an indicator of what the future may hold oscillates between trust and distrust – both vis-à-vis the overall political system and in regard to individual politicians and political parties. Following Luhmann (2000: 97), the overall system generally requires confidence (*Zuversicht*), a trusting attitude that takes itself for granted: »every morning you leave the house without a weapon!« Supporting individual politicians, however, requires trust (*Vertrauen*), an attitude of actively choosing one object of trust over another – risking that you »eventually regret your trusting choice« (Luhmann 2000: 98). The available data reveals that the young men from the urban socio-economic margins involved in urban upheavals did not have much confidence in the overall system, neither in England nor in Guinea. But while the English youth also had no trust in individual politicians, some of the Guineans did. This, I will argue, has to do with different modalities of political inclusion and exclusion. While the English rioters were, in the sense of Luhmann, systematically excluded from politics, their Guinean counterparts could hope for a possible future of being integrated into the political apparatus. However rare, ambiguous, fragile and short-lived their ties with politicians were, there was a slight possibility that their political actions could eventually improve their individual lives, whereas for English rioters, politics largely seemed inaccessible and likely to remain the same – at least from what we know. In that regard, this chapter critically reviews two interrelated tropes that frequently arise in discussions on global

---

3 | My translation from German: »die Möglichkeit, Politik zu beobachten, [bietet] einen Ersatz für die verbaute Möglichkeit, Zukunft zu beobachten. Das Unbekanntsein, die Unbeobachtbarkeit der Zukunft ist deshalb die Bedingung des hohen Aufmerksamkeitswertes der Politik. Das könnte nicht zuletzt erklären, daß die Beobachtung der Politik zwischen Vertrauen und Mißtrauen oszilliert. Keine der beiden Möglichkeiten kann prinzipiell ausgeschlossen werden, da die Politik gleichsam als Statthalter der verborgenen, unerkennbaren Zukunft funktioniert.«

politics: the trope of inclusive democracies in Europe, and the trope of the marginalised urban underclass in Africa.

## The 2011 England Riots: The Absent Future

The England riots ensued shortly after a Metropolitan Police Service officer shot 29-year-old Marc Duggan on 4 August, 2011. Two days later, Duggan's relatives and local residents requested information on the circumstances of his death in front of the Tottenham police station. The demonstration later turned into a standoff between police and protesters (Scott 2011), which sparked the riots that spread with unprecedented speed across London and to other cities (Newburn 2014). Five people lost their lives; 2584 shops were looted, and the overall financial cost is estimated at around half a billion pounds sterling (Riots, Communities and Victims Panel 2012: 3). While the London Metropolitan Police Service (2012: 14) described the five days of rioting as »unprecedented in the capital's history«, British Prime Minister David Cameron was quick to emphasise the banality of the event. »This was not political protest, or a riot about protest or politics,« he argued, »it was common-or-garden [ordinary] thieving, robbing and looting« (House of Commons 2011). In a sense, Cameron was right: the English rioters of 2011 had no connection whatsoever to networks and symbols that we tend to call ›political‹. The rioters were not associated with political parties (the opposition equally condemned the riots), not organised in any legible way (see Williams 2012) and, most importantly, they made no reference to the future. Even those who most violently confronted the state's security forces did not, according to their own reports, imagine a different politics to come.

One of the most detailed independent inquiries into the rioters' motivations is the ›Reading the Riots‹ report, produced by a collaborative research team from the London School of Economics and the Guardian newspaper (Lewis et al. 2011). Based on interviews with 270 people who claimed that they were involved in the riots, it constitutes a central empirical reference in various sociological and criminological analyses (e.g. Body-Gendrot 2013; Slater 2011; Sutterlüty 2014; Valluvan, Kapoor and Kalra 2013; for critiques, see Henri and Hutnyk 2013: 210-213; Treadwell et al. 2013: 2, 4). Their observations match with various others' in that they see rioters as largely apathetic vis-à-vis the political future.⁴ A 19-year-old unemployed man from Birmingham, for example, shrugs when asked what he would like to see change: »Fuck knows, dunno, don't really care about that no more. I've gone past caring. Just think there's no point in me wishing, wanting things to happen« (Lewis et al. 2011: 26). The rioters' fatalism was highlighted in all other large-scale empirical analyses (Morrell et al. 2011: 34-35; Riots, Communities and Victims Panel 2012: 8). In fact, the ›future‹ appeared in reports exclusively to designate what the rioters ›lacked‹, what they had lost faith in. Rather than struggling for a better future, rioters seemed far more concerned with either the past (when framing the riots as taking revenge on the police) or the present (when describing the riots in terms of situational excitement and looting opportunities). A rioter called Daniel said he was striving for revenge:

I was there for revenge and I will always remember the day when *we* had the police and the government scared. For once, they were the ones living on the edge, they, like, *they* felt how *we* felt, they felt threatened by us. That was the best three days of my life. (The Guardian 2011)

Daniel and his friends were on holiday when their peers in London sent them Blackberry messages with images of the riots. They immediately cut their holidays short and came back to England nine days earlier than planned.

I always *thought* to myself when I was on holiday: ›Well, this chance may never come again.‹ I saw it as my opportunity, like, *now* was the opportunity to get revenge. It wasn't even just the police, just the whole government, like, everything they do, they make things harder for us, like, they make it hard for us to get jobs, even when, like, we do get benefits, they cut it down. (The Guardian 2011)

Daniel's comment that »this chance may never come again«, as well as the narrative of ›payback‹, exemplify that the riots were indeed no attempt at

---

**4 |** To name but a few examples, Sutterlüty (2014: 49) remarks »it is highly significant that they hardly spoke of hopes«; Body-Gendrot (2013: 18) speaks of »futureless young males«; and Lewis et al. (2011: 26) argue that »many [rioters] felt that little was likely to change«. All available data from interviews that I have been able to gather confirm this view.

political reform. As much as the »mayhem saw rioters take control back, in their own minds, from the clutches of the police« (Lewis et al. 2011: 20), this reversal of police dominance was known to be short-lived and did not aim at future improvements in policing or socio-economic redistribution. However, within the moment, the reversal of established power relations provoked great enthusiasm. Daniel proudly recalls: »We actually had the choice of letting officers off the hook or seriously injuring them. Like, I threw a brick at a policewoman, I saw her drop; I could have just easily bricked her again. I didn't because it was a woman« (The Guardian 2011).

Looting accounted for half of all riot-related crimes (Riots, Communities and Victims Panel 2012: 17); many commentators distinguished it as the England riots' essential feature (see Bauman 2011; Moxon 2011; Riots, Communities and Victims Panel 2012; Stuart Hall in Williams 2012; Žižek 2011). Looting generally appears to take place within a highly present-centred atmosphere (Collins 2008: 247). A business student who claimed to have made £2,500 by looting, recalls a sense of urgency: »I wanna get it now. I want it now. That's what it was« (Lewis et al. 2011: 29). Karl, a young man interviewed during the riots by Treadwell et al. (2013: 11), explains:

I am 23, never had no job [...]. I got fuck all [nothing] to lose man, fucking Babylon [police] can't do shit anyway, fuck them. We run this town now, not them pricks man, I am gonna take as much as I can get. I want to get watches man, I want me a fucking Rolex.

A looter going by the name of G explains: »Opportunities come and you can't let them go, know what I'm saying?« (Treadwell et al. 2013: 5).

Often the two key motives – revenge against the police, and looting – seemed to intertwine within an effervescent »party atmosphere« (see Lewis et al. 2011; Morrell et al. 2011; Treadwell et al. 2013). Rioters enjoyed what Collins (2008: 250) calls a »moral holiday«, which created a sense of social solidarity amongst the marginalised social strata. Daniel, an English white man in his thirties, recalls a »bonfire atmosphere« with people cheering him on when he set a police car on fire: «I felt great and excited ›Yeah, fuck them, fuck them scum bastards‹ [...]. It was just an opportunity. I never set fire to a police car before. [...] It's a police car, I know what they stand for« (The Guardian 2011).

The rioters came from a disadvantaged socio-economic background: approximately 59 per cent of the riot suspects were amongst the poorest 20 per cent of the national population; 76 per cent had a previous caution or conviction, and 63 per cent were from ethnic minorities (Lewis et al. 2011: 5; Riots, Communities and Victims Panel 2012: 18; Ministry of Justice 2012; Slater 2011). But even though 85 per cent of the 270 rioters interviewed by Lewis et al. (2011: 13) said that policing and police discrimination were a key cause for the riots, the riots themselves featured almost no reference at all to police racism or to the preceding protests over the death of Marc Duggan. Some rioters rejected outright the notion of political protests. A rioter going by the name of Dexter explicitly exclaimed: »Fucking protests, what, the riots? Like the lads from round here are gonna bother going up town for a protest! It was for 10 pairs of free Adidas. It's a fucking joke [to claim that this was a protest], anyone can see it's fucking fantasy« (Treadwell et al. 2013: 11-12). This seems puzzling, for upheavals are commonly seen as inherently political in the sense that they threaten the stability of the political system and insofar as regimes become vulnerable when they are forced to demonstrate their power, in particular consensual democracies that execute physical force against their own citizens (see Luhmann 2002: 47-48). Why, then, did none of the English rioters seize the moment and make future-related political demands, although they would have had plenty of reasons to do so? And why did the political opposition, notably the Labour Party, refrain from politicising the riots to a greater degree?

Along the lines of Niklas Luhmann's systems theory, we can explore the underlying issues in terms of political inclusion and exclusion. If rioters did not communicate in the language of politics, that is, if they made no future-related political demands, it means that they were not included in the political system. Although Luhmann can only illuminate the excluding political system and not the perspectives of the excluded individuals themselves – a problematic theoretical stance, to which I return below – his focus on inclusion and exclusion highlights the boundaries of politics and, more symbolically, the boundaries of who can or cannot participate in the contest of different futures. These boundaries were stark and systemic in the English case, while they were fuzzy and porous in Guinea. This is because, in the English case, political parties depend fundamentally on the systematic procedures of electoral democracy. They had little interest in considering a riot as being political – if they had done so, they would have aimed for systemic suicide. Instead, the familiar political order was to be restored as swiftly as possible to dissipate any doubts about the system's authority and the political parties' legitimacy in representing the will of the people. Indeed, that is precisely what happened. The English security and judicial apparatus reacted with an »extraordinary« effort to criminalise the rioters as quickly as possible (Newburn 2014: 20), organising 1,200 riot-related hearings before magistrates within ten days of the riots, which resulted in all-night sittings across the country and led to sentences that were generally two-to-three-times longer than usual (Slater 2011). By March 2012, the Metropolitan Police Service (MPS) had made 4,000 riot-related arrests and their investigations still occupied over 411 officers at a cost of £33.5 million, many of them analysing the 200,000 hours of surveillance-camera footage (Metropolitan Police Service 2012: 126, 128-29). The MPS is currently developing a ›Digital Imagery Strategy‹ with video surveillance technology to respond »to any future large-scale public disorder in London«, at an estimated cost of £43 million (Metropolitan Police Service 2012: 128-29). In short, the English political system has not only a strong interest but also a high capacity to exclude the disaffected urban margins from politics.

The upshot for the national population, according to Luhmann, is straightforward. Whoever wants to be included in the political system needs to display confidence in that arrangement, and they need to trust specific politicians for whom they can vote. Otherwise, given the absence of feasible alternatives, »one can only feel unhappy and complain about it«, or organise »protests that won't change anything« (Luhmann 2000: 103; Luhmann 1996). The risks of this arrangement seem manageable for the English political system. Although the lack of trust amongst the voting public might eventually diminish the size of the system through a dearth of participation (Luhmann 2000: 104), and although there is evidence for gradually decreasing political participation among young and poor voters in the UK (Flinders 2014), the turnout in the 2015 elections was still higher than in all three previous elections. And while the public's lack of confidence »may have indirect repercussions on the political system«, it will first and foremost affect those who lack confidence, thereby causing »feelings of alienation« and a »retreat into smaller worlds, [...] fundamentalist attitudes or other forms of retotalizing milieux and ›life-worlds‹« (Luhmann 2000: 103-104). Whether these life-worlds will gain political relevance in the future remains to be seen. In the case of organised gangs during the 2011 England riots, which can indeed be understood as life-worlds (see Hazen and Rodgers 2014; Venkatesh 2006), that was not the case. Although 19 per cent of the arrested rioters were gang members and »otherwise hostile gangs suspended ordinary hostilities« or even collaborated during the riots (Lewis et al. 2011: 21, 22), they remained politically illegible and, in the long term, did not disrupt the system's stability. Quite to the contrary, police emerge today as an even stronger political-administrative sub-system than before, and criminalisation of rioters has easily excluded them from various social systems at once – a trans-systemic exclusion that systems theory is at great pains to explain (on *Kopplung*, see Luhmann 1995a: 407-495).

In sum, Luhmann can explain why the political system excludes rioters and refrains from politicising them, yet he cannot explain why they made no political demands. More broadly, this shows that thinking in terms of functionally differentiated social systems makes sense from within these systems, but much less sense from outside these systems. This applies in particular to concerns of intersectionality (for a recent discussion, see Collins 2015). For those who are simultaneously excluded from various social systems – the jobless, less-educated, and criminalised poor with no political party to vote for – the issue is social exclusion *tout court* (see Depelchin 2005: 210; Grizelj and Biti 2014: 14). When Luhmann (1995b; 1996) explored this concern of total social exclusion after a visit to Brazil's *favelas*, the German theorist, who is usually known for his unemotional and anti-normative style of theorising, was visibly troubled by the magnitude of exclusion, which, he argued, eschewed all description and explanation. He seems to unwittingly refer to himself when writing:

> To the surprise of all well-meaning [people], one has to notice that there is exclusion after all; in fact it is plentiful and in a form of wretchedness that eludes all description. Anyone who dares to visit the South American urban *favelas* and gets out alive can give account of this. But even a visit of the neighbourhoods affected by the shutdown of coal mining in Wales may suffice. It needs no empirical investigations. Whoever believes their eyes can see it, in fact in an impressiveness that all explanations fail to convey. (Luhmann 1996: 227)[5]

---

**5** | My translation from German: »Zur Überraschung aller Wohlgesinnten muß man feststellen, daß es doch Exklusionen gibt, und zwar massenhaft und in einer Art von Elend, *die sich der Beschreibung entzieht*. Jeder, der einen Besuch in den Favelas südamerikanischer Großstädte wagt und lebend wieder herauskommt, kann davon berichten. Aber schon ein Besuch in den Siedlungen, die die Stillegung des Kohlebergbaus in Wales hinterlassen hat, kann davon überzeugen. Es

It is revealing when a constructivist theorist asks the reader to simply ›believe their eyes‹, as if reality was suddenly a more simple, immediate matter. What it actually implies is that Luhmann's approach cannot make sense of the perspectives it excludes. The agency of the excluded, and more specifically the ›absent future‹ in protests and riots, inevitably requires a different frame of analysis.

Research on urban youth and politics in African Studies can contribute significantly to such an approach (e.g. Abbink 2005; Branch and Mampilly 2015; Christiansen, Utas and Vigh, 2006; Christensen and Utas 2008; Diouf 2003; El-Kenz 1996; Vigh 2010; Zghal 1995). Branch and Mampilly (2015: 35), for instance, argue that among the protesting urban underclass, the »horizon for political action is now: it is all or nothing, because faith in the possibility of reform requires faith that the state will follow through on its promises.« Such confidence in the state is largely absent at the urban margins, which makes voicing political demands rather absurd for them, and helps to explain why their protests are so often interlaced with looting. Just as political and economic exclusion seem to go hand-in-hand – at least from the perspective of the excluded (Branch and Mampilly 2015: 7) – upending the political order inevitably constitutes a rare opportunity to seize the material goods that usually remain out of reach under that order. Getting something tangible and material out of a protest may be prioritised over making future-related political demands, not just amongst the poorest rioters but equally amongst those who have lost hope that the political order is going to change. As in the England riots, rioters will join the carnivalesque exceptionality not to seek political inclusion, but to settle accounts from the past or to cash in on the present. If the political system, in Luhmann's (2002: 169) words, functions as the governor (*Statthalter*) of an unknown tomorrow, the English rioters simply enjoyed their limited control over the now (if only for five days). As the Guinean case indicates, the future becomes much more of a resource among urban marginal youth when political inclusion and exclusion are less distinct and definitive.

---

bedarf dazu keiner empirischen Untersuchungen. Wer seinen Augen traut, kann es sehen, und zwar *in einer Eindrücklichkeit, an der die verfügbaren Erklärungen scheitern.*«

## Guinea in 2009: The Imminent Future

In August 2009, the Guinean military junta ›Conseil National pour la Démocratie et le Développement‹ (CNDD) had been in power for nine months. Their bloodless coup in December 2008, which followed the death of former President Lansana Conté, had been widely applauded by the national population (McGovern 2009). However, criticism and impatience increased among the Guinean public when the junta delayed preparations for the democratic elections which they had promised. Many wondered whether the junta's president Dadis Camara would stick to the transition timeframe and keep his promise not to run for president in the elections. The political climate was tense. Since the 2007 general strike, which had featured countrywide demonstrations and violent clashes on an unprecedented scale (see Engeler 2008), tightly organised youth groups – so-called ›staffs‹, ›clans‹ and ›gangs‹ – had become important mobilisers for contentious politics, rallying masses of underemployed urban youth to join protests, political gatherings and demonstrations in Guinea's capital city Conakry (Philipps 2013a). Politicians were eager to attract large crowds through these groups, be it in an effort to undermine the state's fragile monopoly of power or, conversely, to undergird it. In 2009, different political movements made their proposed political futures seem propitious and accessible to these gangs, clans and staffs, and this future depended notably on President Dadis Camara: the ›Mouvement Dadis Doit Partir‹ (MDDP) proclaimed that ›Dadis has to leave‹, while the ›Mouvement Dadis Doit Rester‹ (MDDR) argued that ›Dadis has to stay‹. Middlemen, shifting between the ghetto and party headquarters, brokered deals between youth groups and politicians. Partisan politics intertwined with ghetto discourses, money handouts and promises for a brighter future. A language of imminent change permeated the urban margins of Conakry. It was believed that, after the 2007 general strike had failed to democratise the country, the coming elections would; and also that the youth would be employed in the state that they were about to capture.

Junta leader Dadis Camara was the most explicit in seeking the support of Conakry's ›ghetto youth‹. In August 2009 he organised a mass rally at Kaporo Rails, a symbolic site of an earlier state-society conflict in Conakry. He channelled money to 37 leaders of different staffs and clans in Conakry, and gave a passionate speech, in which he declared solidarity with the axis area's ghetto youth: »If they call you thugs,« Camara exclaimed, »me too,

I deem myself a thug!« I attended the rally at Kaporo Rails with Dogg Mayo. One of my first informants, Dogg Mayo was an agitated man in his late twenties, an Islamic Studies student in his final year of university, and the *conseiller* of the staff ›Bunker Family‹. As a *conseiller*, he would, amongst other things, negotiate with middlemen from political parties about whether or not to support them in demonstrations, rallies and in organising protests in their favour. They would sit together, negotiate prices, condemn political corruption and injustice, and assert the need for radical political change. Dogg Mayo thereby occupied a paradoxical position in Conakry's politics. On the one hand, he was a self-proclaimed ghetto youth, proudly representing in sartorial styles, gestures and rap-inspired vocabulary the transnational margins of an urban world, to which many English rioters would probably also count themselves.[6] At the same time, he also transcended these margins because he was also linked to the very politicians at the centre of national power that he despised as the corrupt elite. Dogg Mayo's position thus oscillated between inclusion and exclusion, allowing for an agency »outside of increasingly outmoded laws and regulatory systems«, as Simone (1998: 84) puts it, and bespeaking an urbanity of »nonformalized, creolized, hodgepodged social orders and territories [that] obscure any clear reading of what is going on« (Simone 1998: 83). More specifically, Dogg Mayo's political position represents the connections that were possible within the Guinean context of 2009 between the urban margins and the national political centre. It was through such connections that the political future could become an important resource for youth at the urban margins.

In early August 2009, Dogg Mayo had co-organised Dadis Camara's rally and mobilised the Bunker Family staff to attend his speech. After the speech, Dogg Mayo approached me with an air of absolute confidence.

---

**6 |** Socio-economically marginalised, sometimes ethnically discriminated against, and frequently in conflict with the law, the English rioters shared important characteristics that the Guinean young men I interviewed between 2009 and 2012 mostly used to describe themselves. Both cases of protests and riots were associated with global hip-hop culture (on Guinea, see Philipps 2013a; on England, see Hancox 2011), and rap songs like the UK's Lethal Bizzle song (2007) ›Babylon‹s burning down the Ghetto', which made allusions to the likelihood of urban riots in England four years before 2011, convey the same narratives that Guinea's ghetto youth evoked in interviews.

»I'm telling you, this is someone, a man, who is patriotic! He himself is a *patriot*!! [...] And the transition timeframe that he promised once more: he will respect it. This is someone who is honest!« Interestingly, the president had not mentioned the transition timeframe at all during his speech and had made no remarks concerning his candidacy during the promised elections – Dogg Mayo had made this part up, eager perhaps to pin his hopes on something substantial. But this was in vain: just five days after the event, I looked for Dogg Mayo and met his friends in a crowded bar, all of whom were gathered around a small television set. The evening news was on; Dadis Camara gave another speech, and rumour had it that he would present himself in the presidential elections. Among the young men there seemed to be a sense of disorientation: noise, laughter, loud political comments of all kinds, a venting of frustrations, criticism, fears, all circulating under the corrugated iron roof. Different voices with entirely dissimilar comments: »Fuck the CNDD!« »And if Dadis does *not* run for president, *they* will make him run.« »Nobody has money nowadays. Everybody is scared. I'm scared, I swear.« »I'm leaving, I'm going back to my home village.« Another assured: »It's just the beginning for now, we will follow and see.« I heard that youth had started to put up barricades to block traffic in the adjacent neighbourhood of Bambéto – signalling that anti-government protests were about to start. Somebody asserted: »By God, if I go out on the streets now, the whole neighbourhood of Kaporo Rails will rise up.« All around, politicians' names were mentioned in relation to corruption scandals; numbers were bandied around the room, claiming that the CNDD had seized SOBRAGUI (the national beer brewery) and that the army drank for free ever since its capture of power – owing the brewery 7 billion Guinean Francs (US$1.5 million). »It's not only Cellou Dallein who ate the Guineans' money. All the ministers, they all ate it.«[7] Another said: »Cellou Dallein is an asshole, a *bastard*.« And yet another: »I'm with Cellou. I'm with Cellou.« »Alpha Condé is an international employee. He's not even married.«[8] Somebody approached me: »Wait, you there, which candidate have you seen who can do something here

---

[7] | Cellou Dallein is a Guinean opposition politician of the Union des Forces Démocratiques de Guinée (UFDG). He was a minister under Lansana Conté and is president Alpha Condé's main opponent today.

[8] | Alpha Condé is Guinea's current president and a long-time opposition politician heading the Rassemblement du Peuple de Guinée (RPG).

in Guinea? *Who?*« And while I stuttered something about how youth can transform the country, somebody else said: »My father is not even a politician. I haven't been to school. I don't even know politics.«

Later that night, I found Dogg Mayo in front of the television watching Dadis Camara's speech. »I *really* loved this guy,« he confessed. »I loved him in the beginning. But now, with these rumours that he wants to run for president....« He looked at the set: »Now he's talking about the underclass! If he speaks to us about the underclass, we will *shit* on him! You're for the underclass? Then help the underclass!« And when I started emphasising again my amazement at »all these people who are ready to change the country,« Dogg Mayo interrupted me harshly, as if my comment could have implied any sort of doubt:

Oh, we're ready to change this country! If we weren't ready to change – me, whom you see in front of you, if someone gives me money, even if it's 100,000 Guinean Francs [equivalent to US$20 at the time], he hands me a gun with – how do you say? With *ammunition*, I am ready to kill. Now, *wallahi*, I kill. ›Cause this one [gesturing towards Dadis Camara on television] does *not* want us to change. Even if in our lives, there is no more hope; but our children to come: that guy still wants our children to live the same lives as us. He's just gotta fuck himself! We are sick and tired of military regimes. [...] Those guys can't do nothing. They don't have any more power than that gang of Lansana Conté.[9] We faced them! And back then, people didn't have guns. [...] People will be *very well* prepared this time before taking to the streets.

Indeed, the wave of protests that started that very night in August 2009 can be regarded as the beginning of the end of Dadis Camara's presidency, and later of the CNDD regime itself. Several demonstrations and protests led up to the notorious massacre on 28 September, 2009 by Guinea's security forces, killing at least 150 demonstrators at an opposition rally in Conakry. Isolated internationally and dreaded by Guineans, the junta crumbled due to internal strife. Dadis was later shot and severely injured by his aide, whom he had held responsible for the massacre. The junta's third-in-command, Sékouba Konaté, took power; and Guinea held presidential elections in 2010, and again in 2015.

---

**9** | Ex-president Lansana Conté ruled Guinea from 1984 to 2008.

Even though the political changes have thus far not improved the livelihoods of Dogg Mayo and his peers, it is crucial here to acknowledge how strongly the rumours about Dadis Camara's plans to run for president seemed to affect the young men in the Kaporo Rails bar, instantaneously causing a diversity of reactions: a young man thinks aloud about moving back to his native village out of fear; a search for new political affiliations begins: who is the politician to trust now? Who has not been corrupt in the past? Given that Conakry's ghetto youth are often depicted as either opportunistic (in that they support the politician who offers them money), merely violent for the fun of it (and for the economic benefits of looting), or ethnically affiliated (to politicians with close ties to their respective neighbourhood), this reaction is remarkable for the heterogeneity of political opinions and its inconclusiveness.

In Luhmann's (2000: 97) terms, the incident constitutes an event that contradicts »previous trusting relationships [and] may lead to a sudden collapse of confidence or trust.« Trust in ›Dadis‹ indeed collapsed and led to overt confusion about the future. Dogg Mayo, after having vented his indignation vis-à-vis the televised image of the president, confesses: »I don't understand, I just don't understand anymore, my brother. I can't understand, I don't know where this is going with this regime. We thought that guy [Dadis Camara] was good.« But the confusion did not last long, as Dogg Mayo simply entered new networks once others failed. Just one week after having organised the rally for the president, he quickly joined the opposition and participated in anti-government demonstrations in late August and September 2009, burning tyres and throwing stones at the police. He was present at the September 28-massacre but escaped unharmed. He claimed to have voted for president Alpha Condé in 2010, the only opposition candidate who had never been part of previous governments. But Condé also betrayed his trust, so he sided with the new opposition, for which he mobilised Kaporo Rails' youth through the networks of Bunker Family. In 2013 Dogg Mayo was still as infuriated by Guinean politics as when I had first met him. He reasserted his hopes of an armed rebellion against the »vampires« who sucked dry the state and continuously emphasised the inevitability of fundamental political change. His thinking about the world around him remained anchored in the future. The future constituted a space of untainted hope, a refuge from the present and, perhaps most importantly, a locus of observation. Perceived from the future, the past lost its powerful grip on reality (»Ahhha! Those fifty years we went through, that's over!«) and, in contrast to the past, the imagined future confirmed Dogg Mayo's political hopes, independent of whatever individual politicians would concoct. As he said in 2009, »if he [Dadis Camara] accepts positively, we change; if he doesn't accept positively, we will change. Because it must change.« In short, the future's quality resided precisely in the fact that it was untamed by reality and fully manipulable by imagination.

Dogg Mayo in that regard seems to exemplify what young militia-men in neighbouring Guinea-Bissau call *dubriagem* – in French: *se débrouiller* (Vigh 2010). Etymologically, *se débrouiller* is related to *brouillard* (fog) and »indicates a process of gaining clarity whilst moving in an opaque (social) environment« (Vigh 2010: 150). Young militia-men in Guinea-Bissau, Vigh (2010: 151) argues, navigate such opaque environments through »a dual temporality« which interrelates »both the socially *immediate* (present) and the socially *imagined* (future).« Differently from more stable social contexts, where the present constitutes the stable basis from where to think about the future, in the case of Bissau's militias the present is as much clarified by the imagined future as the future is imagined through the given possibilities of the present. Knowing how quickly things can change, the political future is thought of as volatile and manipulable and, therefore, as being susceptible to hopeful imaginations, not least to dissipate the distress, confusion and haze of the present. *Dubriagem*, then, is much more than economic survival; it is »a process of disentanglement from (present and future) confining structures and relations as well as a drawing of a line of flight into an envisioned future« (Vigh 2010: 151).

## SUMMARY

This chapter has addressed the uncertain collective future as a key concern and resource of politics (Luhmann 2002; Mitchell 2014). It has inquired into the circumstances in which this becomes a resource for youth at the urban margins, and has thereby turned it into a question of political inclusion and exclusion. I have sketched out two contexts of riots and protests where youth from the urban margins actively destabilised the present political order, yet responded differently to whether their actions aimed at a different future. In the English case from 2011, according to secondary sources the political future remained outside the purview of rioters. The rioters did not voice demands for a better future, and English politicians did not see the upheavals as being political in nature, mainly because they did not depend on the rioters to access or remain in power. That situation was fundamentally different in the Guinean context of 2009, where both the government and the opposition were eager to harness Conakry's urban margins for popular support. Dogg Mayo and his peers could develop political leverage on the basis of an uncertain political future and comparatively inclusive political networks. As mobilisers and participants in political rallies, demonstrations, protests and riots, they would call for imminent political change as *their* project, and they hoped that their actions would tangibly improve their personal lives. Finally, in the dynamic and quickly changing political context of Conakry in 2009, the envisioned future significantly illuminated their understanding of an unstable present. As a utopian space of manipulable realities, the future provided orientation where the present proved either too intangible or too grim to work with on their way forward.

## Bibliography

Abbink, Jon. 2005. »Being Young in Africa: The Politics of Despair and Renewal.« In *Vanguards or Vandals. Youth, Politics and Conflict in Africa*, edited by Jon Abbink and Ineke van Kessel. Leiden: Brill. 1–34.

Akram, Sadiya. 2014. »Recognizing the 2011 United Kingdom Riots as Political Protest A Theoretical Framework Based on Agency, Habitus and the Preconscious.« *British Journal of Criminology* 54(3): 375–392.

Bauman, Zygmunt. 2011. »The London Riots – On Consumerism Coming Home to Roost.« *Social Europe*. Retrieved 9 January, 2015. [http://www.socialeurope.eu/2011/08/the-london-riots-on-consumerism-coming-home-to-roost]

Body-Gendrot, Sophie. 2013. »Urban Violence in France and England: Comparing Paris (2005) and London (2011).« *Policing and Society* 23(1): 6–25.

Branch, Adam, Zachariah Mampilly. 2015. *Africa Uprising: Popular Protest and Political Change*. London: Zed Books.

Christiansen, Catrine, Mats Utas, Henrik E. Vigh (eds.). 2006. *Navigating Youth, Generating Adulthood: Social Becoming in an African Context*. Uppsala: Nordic Africa Institute.

Christensen, Maya, Mats Utas. 2008. »Mercenaries of Democracy: The ›Politricks‹ of Remobilized Combatants in the 2007 General Elections, Sierra Leone.« *African Affairs* 107(429): 515–539.

Collins, Patricia Hill. 2015. »Intersectionality's Definitional Dilemmas.« *Annual Review of Sociology* 41: 1-20.

Collins, Randall. 2008. *Violence: A Micro-Sociological Theory.* Princeton: Princeton University Press.

Comaroff, Jean, John L. Comaroff. 2012a. *Theory from the South. Or, How Euro-America Is Evolving toward Africa.* London: Paradigm Publishers.

Comaroff, Jean, John Comaroff. 2012b. »Theory from the South: A Rejoinder.« *Cultural Anthropology Online.* Retrieved 19 December, 2015. [http://www.culanth.org/fieldsights/273-theory-from-the-south-a-rejoinder]

Cooper, Elizabeth, David Pratten (eds.). 2015. *Ethnographies of Uncertainty in Africa.* Basingstoke: Palgrave Macmillan.

Depelchin, Jacques. 2005. *Silences in African History: Between the Syndromes of Discovery and Abolition.* Dar es Salaam: Mkuki na Nyota Publishers.

Diouf, Mamadou. 2003. »Engaging Postcolonial Cultures: African Youth and Public Space.« *African Studies Review* 46(2): 1–12.

El-Kenz, Ali. 1996. »Youth and Violence.« In *Africa Now: People, Policies and Institutions,* edited by Stephen Ellis. The Hague: Ministry of Foreign Affairs. 42–57.

Engeler, Michelle. 2008. »Guinea in 2008: The Unfinished Revolution.« *Politique africaine* (112): 87–98.

Grizelj, Mario, Vladimir Biti. 2014. *Riskante Kontakte: Postkoloniale Theorien und Systemtheorie?* Berlin: Kulturverlag Kadmos.

Hancox, Dan. 2011. »Rap Responds to the Riots: ›They Have to Take Us Seriously.‹« *The Guardian,* August 12. Retrieved 19 December, 2015. [http://www.theguardian.com/music/2011/aug/12/rap-riots-professor-green-lethal-bizzle-wiley]

Hazen, Jennifer M., Dennis Rodgers. 2014. *Global Gangs: Street Violence across the World.* Minneapolis: University of Minnesota Press.

Henri, Tom, John Hutnyk. 2013. »Contexts for Distraction.« *Journal for Cultural Research* 17(2): 198–215.

House of Commons. 2011. »Standing Order No.13, 11 August.« Retrieved 19 December, 2015. [http://www.publications.parliament.uk/pa/cm201011/cmhansrd/cm110811/debtext/110811-0001.htm]

Lethal Bizzle. 2007. *Babylon's Burning The Ghetto*. Retrieved 19 December, 2015. [https://www.youtube.com/watch?v=hbf83rLG2mQ]

Lewis, Paul et al. 2011. *Reading the Riots: Investigating England's Summer of Disorder*. London: The London School of Economics and Political Science; and The Guardian. Retrieved 17 August, 2014. [http://www.guardian.co.uk/uk/series/reading-the-riots]

Luhmann, Niklas. 1995a. *Das Recht Der Gesellschaft*. Frankfurt am Main: Suhrkamp.

Luhmann, Niklas. 1995b. »Inklusion Und Exklusion.« In *Soziologische Aufklärung 6: Die Soziologie und der Mensch*. Opladen: Westdeutscher Verlag. 237–264.

Luhmann, Niklas. 1996. »Jenseits von Barbarei.« In *Modernität und Barbarei. Soziologische Zeitdiagnose am Ende des 20. Jahrhundert*, edited by M. Miller and H.-G. Soeffner. Frankfurt: Suhrkamp. 219–230.

Luhmann, Niklas. 2000. »Familiarity, Confidence, Trust: Problems and Alternatives.« In *Trust: Making and Breaking Cooperative Relations*, edited by D. Gambetta. Oxford: Basil Blackwell. 94–107.

Luhmann, Niklas. 2002. *Die Politik der Gesellschaft*. Frankfurt am Main: Suhrkamp.

Mbembe, Achille, Sarah Nuttall. 2004. »Writing the World from an African Metropolis.« *Public Culture* 16(3): 347–372.

McGovern, Mike. 2009. »Exceptional Circumstances and Coups d'Etat.« *African Arguments*. Retrieved 11 November, 2010. [http://africanarguments.org/2009/02/exceptional-circumstances-and-coups-detat]

Merton, Robert K. 1938. »Social Structure and Anomie.« *American Sociological Review* 3(1): 672–682.

Metropolitan Police Service. 2012. *Report 4 Days in August. Strategic Review into the Disorder of August 2011*. London: Metropolitan Police Service. Retrieved 9 January, 2015. [http://de.slideshare.net/nuzhound/metropolitan-police-service-report-4-days-in-august]

Mitchell, Timothy. 2014. »Econometality: How the Future Entered Government.« *Critical Inquiry* 40(4): 479–507.

Morrell, Gareth, Sara Scott, Di McNeish, Stephen Webster. 2011. *The August Riots in England Understanding the Involvement of Young People*. London: National Centre for Social Research.

Moxon, David. 2011. »Consumer Culture and the 2011 ›Riots.‹« *Sociological Research Online* 16(4).

Newburn, Tim. 2014. »The 2011 England Riots in Recent Historical Perspective.« *The British Journal of Criminology* 55(1): 39–64.

Philipps, Joschka. 2011. »Sweet Talk or Street Riots? Education and Political Action by Youths in Conakry, Guinea.« In *Education in Fragile Contexts: Government Practices and Political Challenges*, edited by Heribert Weiland, Kerstin Priwitzer, and Joschka Philipps. Freiburg: Freiburger Beiträge zur Entwicklung und Politik. 131–165.

Philipps, Joschka. 2013a. *Ambivalent Rage: Youth Gangs and Political Protests in Conakry, Guinea*. Paris: Éditions L'Harmattan.

Philipps, Joschka. 2013b. »Youth Gangs and Urban Political Protests. A Relational Perspective on Conakry's ›Axis of Evil‹.« In *Living the City in Africa: Processes of Invention and Intervention*, edited by Veit Arlt, Elísio Macamo, and Brigit Obrist. Zürich: Lit-Verlag. 81–98.

Philipps, Joschka. 2014. »Dealing with Diversity: African Youth Research and the Potential of Comparative Approaches.« *Journal of Youth Studies* (published online): 1–16.

Philipps, Joschka. (Forthcoming.) »Crystallising Contention. Social Movements, Protests and Riots in African Studies.« *Review of African Political Economy*.

Riots, Communities and Victims Panel. 2012. *After the Riots. The Final Report of the Riots Communities and Victims Panel*. London: The Riots Communities and Victims Panel.

Robinson, Jennifer. 2011. »Cities in a World of Cities: The Comparative Gesture.« *International Journal of Urban and Regional Research* 35(1): 1–23.

Scott, Stafford. 2011. »If the Rioting Was a Surprise, People Weren't Looking.« *The Guardian*, August 8. Retrieved 3 February, 2015. [http://www.theguardian.com/commentisfree/2011/aug/08/tottenham-riots-not-unexpected]

Simone, AbdouMaliq. 1998. »Urban Social Fields in Africa.« *Social Text* 56: 71–89.

Slater, Tom. 2011. »From ›Criminality‹ to Marginality: Rioting Against a Broken State.« *Human Geography* 4(3): 106–115.

Sutterlüty, Ferdinand. 2014. »The Hidden Morale of the 2005 French and 2011 English Riots.« *Thesis Eleven* 121(1): 38–56.

The Guardian. 2011. »*It Was a War, and We Had the Police Scared.*« Retrieved 19 December, 2015. [http://www.theguardian.com/uk/video/2011/dec/05/reading-riots-video]

Treadwell, James, Daniel Briggs, Simon Winlow, Steve Hall. 2013. »SHOPOCALYPSE NOW: Consumer Culture and the English Riots of 2011.« *The British Journal of Criminology* 53(1): 1–17.

Utas, Mats. 2014. »›Playing the Game‹: Gang/Militia Logics in War-Torn Sierra Leone.« In *Global Gangs: Street Violence across the World*, edited by J. M. Hazen and D. Rodgers. Minneapolis: University of Minnesota Press. 171–192.

Valluvan, Sivamohan, Nisha Kapoor, Virinder S. Kalra. 2013. »Critical Consumers Run Riot in Manchester.« *Journal for Cultural Research* 17(2): 164–182.

Vigh, Henrik. 2010. »Youth Mobilisation as Social Navigation. Reflections on the Concept of Dubriagem.« *Cadernos de Estudos Africanos* (18-19): 140–164.

Vigh, Henrik. 2015. »Social Invisibility and Political Opacity: On Perceptiveness and Apprehension in Bissau.« In *Ethnographies of Uncertainty in Africa, Anthropology, change and development*, edited by E. Cooper and D. Pratten. Basingstoke: Palgrave Macmillan. 111–128.

Williams, Zoe. 2012. »The Saturday Interview: Stuart Hall.« *The Guardian*, February 11. Retrieved 9 January, 2015. [http://www.theguardian.com/theguardian/2012/feb/11/saturday-interview-stuart-hall/print]

Young, Jock. 2007. »Globalization and Social Exclusion: The Sociology of Vindictiveness and the Criminology of Transgression.« In *Gangs in the Global City: Alternatives to Traditional Criminology*, edited by J. M. Hagedorn. Urbana: University of Illinois Press. 52–93.

Zghal, Abdelkader. 1995. »The ›Bread Riot‹ and the Crisis of the One-Party.« In *African Studies in Social Movements and Democracy*, edited by M. Mamdani and E. Wamba-dia-Wamba. Dakar: Codesria. 99–133.

Žižek, Slavoj. 2011. »Shoplifters of the World Unite.« *London Review of Books*, August 19. Retrieved 9 January, 2015. [http://www.lrb.co.uk/2011/08/19/slavoj-zizek/shoplifters-of-the-world-unite]

© Oumou Traoré

© Bah Diancoumba

# 7 Managing Uncertainty

Youth Unemployment, Responsibilisation and Entrepreneurship Training Programmes in Ethiopia

*Julian Tadesse*

## INTRODUCTION

This chapter looks at Entrepreneurship Training Programmes in Ethiopia, which are aimed at young graduates and other economic actors. I argue that in Ethiopia the ruling regime has to be considered as an important factor in understanding the practices of how young graduates come to terms with the future because it is the regime that shapes the environment in which they have to manoeuvre. Rather than examining the plight of individual entrepreneurs and their role in the country's economy, I analyse these training programmes and the discourse in which they are embedded. Drawing on Michel Foucault's (2000) work on discourse and power/knowledge relations, entrepreneurship is treated as a discursive formation. Consequently I understand entrepreneurship as a specific form of rationality that is located in particular regimes of practice and relations of power. I draw on expert interviews with actors in the field of entrepreneurship training as well as with government officials. In addition, youth policy documents and official discourses disseminated through the websites of international actors and the Ethiopian government are considered.

The developmental project of the Ethiopian state leaves little doubt about the future, in that it imagines uniform development in one direction which is to be managed in a top-down authoritarian mode. Nevertheless, uncertainty persists because the government's developmental agenda closely links individuals to societal progress in general. Youth have been one important focal point in this developmental agenda. Evidence can be found in the massive expansion of the educational system from the end of the 1990s onward (Negash 2006), as well as in more explicit forms of mobilisation through youth organisations and government development programmes (Di Nunzio 2014). In this context, youth unemployment has been identified by the government as a major problem that impedes growth and development. More recently, donor-funded programmes to speed up the development of the private sector have been established, and ›entrepreneurship‹ has become a buzzword around which these programmes are centred. Young graduates and other economic actors are encouraged to join Entrepreneurship Training Programmes.

These training programmes can be seen as an example of how the government seeks to manage heightened expectations regarding the future that are created by an expanding educational system. Drawing on the notion of ›enterprising prudentialism‹ introduced in the works of the sociologist Pat O'Malley (O'Malley 1996; 2000) as well as the conceptualisation of ›responsibilisation‹ as a technology of governance which seeks to cultivate the self-management of social risks (Lemke 2002; Shamir 2008),[1] I suggest that these programmes, and the official discourse surrounding them, shape the context of action in which youth engage with uncertain futures in two ways. First, they shift the moral responsibility for economic insecurity onto young graduates themselves; and second, they recast uncertainty in a more positive light by emphasising it as a business-related risk and arguing for the necessity for entrepreneurial innovation.

---

**1 |** ›Responsibilisation‹ was initially conceptualised in the framework of governmentality studies (see Burchell 1993; O'Malley 1996). Nowadays it is used in a wide range of social sciences such as sociology (see Shamir 2008), anthropology (see Trnka and Trundle 2014), youth studies (see Kelly 2001); for a general overview, see Peters (2016). It refers to a neoliberal governmental logic that seeks to enable subjects to make (free) choices in a setting framed by market-based logic, following which subjects are responsible for their choices; this entails a moralisation of the market – meaning a shift of responsibility for social risks such as illness, unemployment and poverty from the state onto individual actors (Lemke 2002). However by resorting to ›technologies of performance‹, the outcome of individual choices is thought to be shaped according to pre-defined outcomes (Hansson 2014). Different sources of authority, including but not limited to state agencies and non-governmental institutions are involved in the responsibilisation of self-managing subjects (Shamir 2008).

Scholars such as Nikolas Rose (1999) have conceptualised technologies of governance that seek to foster self-responsible enterprising subjects by appealing to their ›freedom‹ to make choices in the context of ›advanced liberal nations‹, and have focused on the question of how citizens are compelled to make ›free‹ decisions in the context of a neoliberal market economy. The present contribution addresses a context in which personal freedoms are limited and state-centred modes of economic and social development are favoured over those of the neoliberal market economy. Nonetheless, the ruling regime in Ethiopia also displays the desire and aspiration to shape the behaviour of populations in order to foster self-responsible subjects. While there is on-going debate over the varied meanings (Ferguson 2010) and multifaceted adoption of neoliberalism outside of the global North (Ong 2006), this chapter does not engage with this debate directly but instead contributes to an ›empirical mapping of governmental rationalities and techniques‹ (Rose, O'Malley and Valverde 2006) in a specific setting. In the Ethiopian case it can be argued that the discursive and practical promotion of ›entrepreneurship‹ serves to reframe a largely economic and structural problem – unemployment – as an attitudinal issue. This paper leaves aside the question of how uncertainties are tamed through the actions of young people; instead, I explore how a government envisions the taming of uncertainty through the framing of the specific subjective practice of creating private enterprise. By looking at these training programmes and the rhetoric that accompanies them, we shall gain insight into the Ethiopian government's attempts of managing an educated mass of unemployed youth and, thereby, of managing the future.

## Entrepreneurship Promotion, International Dynamics and Research Trends

I will begin by briefly discussing the role of international organisations in promoting entrepreneurship; following this I outline a number of general trends in the research on entrepreneurship. As a conclusion I will summarise several specific ideas about entrepreneurship education. Entrepreneurship education refers mostly to its inclusion in the curriculum of higher educational institutions. Nevertheless some of the findings can also be applied to training programmes of the kind I focus on, as I will show throughout. It remains important to point out that research on entrepreneurship is mostly concerned with Western economies. Scholarly articles published in academic journals are dominated by this perspective (Shane 1997), and entrepreneurship as a social and economic phenomenon in other parts of the world remains understudied (Lingelbach et al. 2005).

## International dynamics

The belief that establishing new enterprises contributes to the creation of employment has entrenched the promotion of entrepreneurship into political discourse around the globe (Ogbor 2000). This process is related to larger frames of the contemporary capitalist organisation of society and to the idea that continuous economic growth is both necessary and desirable (Binswanger 2006). Calls for stronger inclusion of entrepreneurship into education have gained momentum since the global financial crisis of the late 2000s. In this context entrepreneurship is portrayed as an avenue to sustain growth in a time that is felt to be increasingly uncertain (Volkmann et al. 2009). Against this background, powerful policy makers such as the World Economic Forum push for the alignment of the private sector and governments in order to foster an entrepreneurially-minded society on a global scale, and young people are designated as a primary target group for entrepreneurial education (World Economic Forum 2009). In regard to the so-called ›developing countries‹, international organisations such as the United Nations Development Programme (UNDP) and the World Bank propose the creation of entrepreneurial ventures as a means for ›poverty alleviation‹ and consider appropriate training programmes as tools with which to achieve this (UNDP 2004; Robb, Valerio and Parton 2014). Both organisations have also heavily invested into the promotion of entrepreneurship in Ethiopia.[2] Studies on such policies in the European context point out that supranational bodies increasingly influence how entrepreneurship education is implemented at the national level (Mahieu 2006). For Ethiopia, Tebeje Molla (2013) has shown how the World Bank has used discursive instruments and technical assistance to influence higher-education reform in the country that includes more elements

---

**2** | The UNDP supports the Entrepreneurship Development Programme (EDP) financially (with US$6 million annually) and technically (UNDP 2013), while the World Bank supports the Women's Entrepreneurship Development Project by providing micro-finance and technical support (US$50 million) (World Bank 2012).

of neoliberal policy, for example the introduction of fees for university students. He has particularly pointed out how ›knowledge-based policy instruments‹ serve as a subtle means to influence national policy and serve to mask unequal power relations between the donor and recipient of such aid (ibid.). In Ethiopia this has led to an increased acceptance of concepts such as human capital formation, that is, the belief that the effective injection of education, health and moral values can bring about long-term economic development. The promotion of entrepreneurship in Ethiopia can be contextualised in such understandings. However, as I show below, notions of development which are specific to Ethiopia must also be taken into consideration because these can significantly transform the implementation of policies and their associated meanings.

## Research trends

The study of entrepreneurship is vast and various theories have been put forward regarding the role of entrepreneurship in economic development. Nevertheless, there is much disagreement on central conceptual questions, such as ›who‹ an entrepreneur is and ›what‹ constitutes entrepreneurship (Amit, Glosten and Muller 1993). In the following I will outline some general trends that have shaped contemporary research on entrepreneurship. The term entrepreneur is ascribed to Richard Cantillon (2015), who already in the eighteenth century described the figure as a risk-taker who makes an investment regardless of the uncertainty of the outcome. Initial research was concerned with answering the question of ›Who is an entrepreneur?‹. Influenced by Joseph Schumpeter's (1912) thoughts, who regarded entrepreneurs as innovators and critical agents of economic change, attempts were made to define the traits and characteristics of the ideal entrepreneur (Berglund 2013: 721). While these attempts remained unsatisfactory (ibid.), they appear to have consolidated discursive patterns that portray the entrepreneur as an exceptional, heroic, male figure (Ogbor 2000) who recognises (economic) opportunities and creates something out of nothing.

As criticism of the ›traits approach‹ mounted, more inclusive concepts of ›the entrepreneur‹ emerged and researchers turned to questions of practice and attempted to describe the process of new business creation (Gartner 1988). The question to be answered shifted to »what the entrepreneur does, and not who the entrepreneur is« (ibid.: 57). In this context, Karin Berglund (2013) points out that contemporary management and entrepreneurship textbooks revolve around the nexus of opportunity recognition, business-plan development and the appropriate managerial techniques which are necessary to achieve success as an entrepreneur. She concludes that the shift to behavioural understandings of entrepreneurial success allows the creation of a discourse that posits ›entrepreneurial competencies‹ as learnable and, therefore, as something that can be achieved by anybody.

## Entrepreneurship education

Entrepreneurship education and entrepreneurship training programmes are based on beliefs that entrepreneurial behaviours can be taught and learned (Fayolle 2007). Instead of tracing the debate on whether these assumptions hold true and what constitutes the appropriate methods of entrepreneurial education, I now outline some of the notions promulgated by mainstream research as well as their critical reception.

The following quote exemplifies how the aims and needs of entrepreneurial education are conceptualised in mainstream research (Miettinen 2003: 4):

The educational system traditionally teaches young people to reproduce facts and to look for work as an employee. Entrepreneurs, in contrast, need an education which gives them attitudes, and skills such as self-motivation, creativity, opportunity seeking and the ability to cope with uncertainty.

Here, entrepreneurship education is set apart from ›traditional‹ Western education, which centres on acquiring knowledge and skills that enable students to find employment. In contrast, entrepreneurship education is portrayed as being focused on attitudinal change and fostering entrepreneurial motivation. Furthermore, it should encourage openness towards opportunity and risk. At its heart, then, lies a ›rhetoric of self-making‹ that extols the embracing of uncertain futures (Bromber et al. 2015). Therefore, in essence entrepreneurship education is not only about learning how to manage a business but also about managing one's own personality (Berglund 2013). Consequently, a ›high level of ideological consensus‹ needs to be enacted upon the individual (Holmgren and From 2008: 387) because the transformation of beliefs and morals in accordance with market demands is a prerequisite for the development of an entrepreneurial identity. Demands for the realisation of the ›enterprising self‹ are not, however, limited to the context of creating new business for its own sake. Behaviour that is assumed to be entrepreneurial in nature comprises attitudes such as flexibility, problem-solving, decision-making and creativity; and these are attributes which are also demanded by the labour market (Brown, Hesketh and Wiliams 2003). In this way these programmes can also be understood as a means of inculcating conformity with the requirements of the labour market into young people's aspirations.

This brief overview of understandings of entrepreneurship has illustrated some particularities I deem pertinent for the framing of my research. First, the promotion of entrepreneurship has to be seen in the context of larger international trends. Second, entrepreneurship education operates within a frame that targets the very understanding of ›who we are‹ by aiming to create an entrepreneurial identity. It thereby devises a managerial approach to economic contingency and the self.

## Political background

The following section provides an overview of the politics of the current Ethiopian regime and its ideological underpinnings. In order to situate the application of entrepreneurship programmes in an Ethiopian setting and to allow a comprehensive understanding of the framing of such programmes, I will further explore how the regime aims to build ties between itself and young people in the country.

### Revolutionary democracy

The current Ethiopian government, led by the Ethiopian People's Revolutionary Democratic Front (EPRDF), has been in power since 1991. Although rooted in a Marxist-Leninist guerrilla movement, the new world order at the end of the Cold War forced the EPRDF to make concessions on political and economic liberalisation in order to secure the support of (Western) donor countries (Bach 2011). As a consequence of this, the Soviet-style planned economy of the previous military regime was dissolved and the state embarked upon a course of ›democratisation‹ as well as administrative and bureaucratic reform. A new constitution was introduced that acknowledged the political and socio-cultural rights of the diverse ethnic groups in Ethiopia under a newly established federal system which was based on ethno-linguistically-defined regions (Abbink 2011). Nonetheless, overall this process was marked only by »selective adhesion to the model of the liberal democracy and free market« (Chinigò and Fantini 2015: 3). Instead, the EPRDF opted to pursue revolutionary democracy (*abyotawi demokrasi* in Amharic) as its core doctrine, which encompasses »a set of governance and power techniques marked by vanguard party rule derived from the Marxist-Leninist tradition« (Hagmann and Abbink 2011: 585) and is fused with liberal elements such as multi-party elections. Beyond this it accords »a dominant role [to] the party-led state in politics, economics and society« (ibid.). Noted for its ambiguity, the resulting ideology has been described as »neither revolutionary, nor democratic« but instead as a flexible device to rationalise the continued political and economic domination of the state by the EPRDF (Bach 2011: 641).

While observers acknowledge the far-reaching socio-political transformation that has taken place under EPRDF rule, they also point to the endurance of authoritarian policies and practices. Critical scholars assert that after more than twenty years in power the EPRDF shows no signs of a serious commitment to political pluralism (Hagmann and Abbink 2011). On the contrary, the past decade was marked by a notable deterioration of civic rights and political freedoms (cf. Human Rights Watch 2010). As examples of this trend observers point to the increased utilisation of legislative tools as well as administrative structures to suppress oppositional politics (Aalen and Tronvoll 2009). The EPRDF-led government in turn emphasises its developmental achievements and points to a decade of sustained double-digit growth to dismiss its critics. Indeed, claims to economic and social development increasingly serve to legitimise the party's continued rule, and the ›democratisation‹ rhetoric of the 1990s has been largely replaced with that of developmentalism. As Marco Di Nunzio (2015: 1187) rightly notes: »The politics of the ruling party, especially at the highest level, is informed by an ideological commitment to development: delivering development and economic growth for the country pervades the sense of mission through which Ethiopian political elites validate and justify their leadership.« This developmental agenda further guarantees the sustained support of donor countries and organisations which the regime has enjoyed for the past two decades, despite its peculiar understanding of democratic processes and rejection of the neoliberal economic model. In fact, the party and its chief ideologue, the late Prime Minister Meles Zenawi, have presented its economic strategy as an alternative to the neoliberal model.

## Developmental capitalism

Since the beginning of the 2000s the EPRDF has subscribed to developmental capitalism (*lematawi habt*) with explicit reference to the model of East Asian developmental states, which accords a central role to the state in economic matters. Outlined in the writings of Meles Zenawi (2012), the adoption of a state-led economic model is argued to represent the only path to economic growth in the context of developing countries. Meles argued that only a strong state could curb the plundering of national resources and steer the private sector towards a productive role, if necessary by threatening to sanction its activities. In its application it defines a context where the EPRDF-led party-state not only maintains control over key economic sectors such as finance, energy and telecommunications, but also actively participates in the economy through a range of parastatal companies and party-affiliated businesses, thereby providing it with a dominant position in the economic domain (Vaughan and Gebremichael 2011).

The domination of the Ethiopian economy by these parastatal companies as well as the business empire of Ethiopian-Saudi billionaire Sheikh Mohammed Hussein Al Amoudi, who is the largest foreign investor in Ethiopia, have led to complaints of ›unfair competition‹ by the remnants of the private sector (ibid.). The relationship between the private sector in general and the ruling party is described as one marked by ›mutual hostility‹ (ibid.).

The EPRDF's hegemonic claim is by no means limited to economic matters – development is conceived of as being a broad, collective endeavour. In the understanding of the party's leadership, the state's role cannot be reduced to fostering economic growth alone but must also include social development because both are mutually contingent. Drawing on Putnam's claims on the positive role of civil society organisations in development processes, Meles Zenawi (2012: 147-8) elaborated that:

Creating the proper blend of norms, values, and rules to reduce uncertainty and transaction costs is a critical factor in accelerated growth and development. [...] It [social development] is created by social activity, by civic engagement in the context of horizontal and dense networks and inculcated and sustained through modeling, socialization and sanctions. The state plays a critical role in social capital accumulation through undermining patronage networks and promoting fairness and equity, through the promotion of participation and democracy, and through the appropriate sanctions and efforts at socialization.

It is noteworthy that here social capital formation is understood as a process largely shaped from above; contrary to Putnam's understanding of the state as an enabler of civic engagement, in the Ethiopian case the state is envisioned to take a leading role in this process. As a consequence scholars do not interpret the developmental ambitions of the Ethiopian government as an end unto itself but rather see it as part of an »ambitious and revolutionary project of social engineering« (Fantini 2013: 6) that complicates the distinction between claims to socio-economic development and »the determination to discipline and control the population« (ibid.) in the name of the development project. In its own terms, however, the EPRDF understands its hegemonic aspirations as a »coalition with the people« (Vaughan 2011). While the party initially focused on mobilising its rural peasant base, it has increasingly thought to incorporate urban populations into its structures as well (ibid.).

## The 2005 elections: Consolidation of state power

Observers consider the 2005 national elections as a decisive turning point towards the formation of the EPRDF as a mass-based political organisation and towards a more vigorous engagement of urban populations, including youth, into its political agenda. Although these elections saw large support for oppositional parties, especially in the urban centres, the EPRDF declared itself the winner of the elections; demonstrators took to the streets in the belief that the incumbent party had rigged the process in its favour (Abbink 2006). The disputed elections were followed by a wide-spread crackdown on the opposition and its supporters. Over 190 people died in clashes with security forces and thousands were arrested, amongst them many young people (ibid.).

After the 2005 elections, the EPRDF began a massive recruitment campaign and overall party membership increased significantly, from 760,000 in 2005 to more than five million in 2010 (Aalen and Tronvoll 2009). Further observers noted the re-establishment of mass associations formed under the legal framework of »civil society organisations« (Vaughan

2011: 634). Through the growing control of neighbourhood councils, local NGOs and public administration, the EPRDF further increased its ability to mobilise and control the electorate (Di Nunzio 2014). Like this it gained an effective monopoly over distributing benefits and could muster support through regulating access to development programmes and employment opportunities (Lefort 2012). In this context, tackling unemployment was deemed to be a major tool for mobilising political support in urban constituencies (Di Nunzio 2015). As a result of this, the number of people more or less directly employed by the state (such as teachers, development agents and health-education workers) grew from around 126,000 in 2005 to over 250,000 by 2010 (Vaughan 2011: 634). Entrepreneurship programmes were established under which unemployed youth were organised into economic cooperatives (Di Nunzio 2015). In the subsequent elections of 2010 and May 2015 the EPRDF further increased its grip on parliament. In the last elections the party officially won every single parliamentary seat, including the single seat that had been held by an opposition politician following the 2010 elections.[3]

## YOUTH POLICY AS AN INSTRUMENT OF STATE REGULATION

To understand how entrepreneurship programmes have become one of the government's most favoured instruments to regulate youth unemployment over the last decade, a closer look at policy towards youth is important. Mayssoun Sukarieh and Stuart Tannock (2011: 683) rightly point out: »Youth [...] is never simply an effect of, but is also a tool and technology for managing social change.« As such it has become a preferred and particularly »productive social category« (ibid.). If youth is to be understood as a social construct it is crucial to recognise that dominant political actors seek to shape this category in ways that support the realisation of their own ideological vision of the future (Sukarieh 2012). Youth policies are one of the sites where youth as a productive social category is envisioned. In the context of the process and intentions of youth policy formulation in post-Soviet transitional societies, Douglas Blum has argued that youth policies

---

[3] | Opposition leaders complained that their followers had been intimidated and that many of their candidates were barred from registering for the elections (Neamin 2015).

contain an »analysis of current problems, designation of operational goals, and concrete plans of action« (Blum 2007: 117) as well as a »vision of governance, including desirable modes of institutionalizing the processes of youth socialization and politicization« (ibid.: 105). Furthermore, such policies frame desirable modes of moral regulation for youth populations from the vantage point of government (ibid.: 117). It follows that youth policy not only serves to facilitate the loyalty of young people in processes of nation building and development but also seeks to establish their active participation. Such policies frequently employ a binary conception of youth so as to distinguish between morally acceptable and deviant behaviour – and this permits the sanctioning of productive behaviour according to the ideological vision of dominant political actors.

Accordingly the EPRDF's stance towards youth has been marked by a duality that at times champions youths as the torch-bearers of development while at other times vilifies them as criminal delinquents. In tune with this the government's discourse on youth ranges from calls for ›empowerment‹ to rhetorics of criminalisation and calls for punishment. Exemplary for the latter is the Vagrancy Control Proclamation No. 384/2004 (known in Amharic as *Ye Adegegna Bozene*), which defines certain youths negatively as persons who »disturb the tranquillity« of society and engage in unlawful and morally unacceptable actions (Gebremariam and Lule 2014). Ostensibly created to tackle problems of juvenile delinquency, this proclamation was later applied to persecute youths who had engaged in oppositional politics (Di Nunzio 2014).

## Ethiopian youth policy

In contrast the first National Youth Policy introduced in the same year is couched in more positive language and places an emphasis on youth potential. It draws on buzzwords from global development discourse when it envisions the creation of »an empowered young generation with a democratic outlook and ideals« (Ministry of Youth, Sports and Culture 2004: 19). It claims that youth issues had been hitherto neglected and that, as a consequence, »youth could [not] actively and effectively participate in the process of national development« (Ministry of Youth, Sports and Culture 2004: 6). The policy further acknowledges the material and social problems faced by young people in Ethiopia, in particular unemployment. Nevertheless it similarly constructs youth as a social category in the binary terms of potential and risk, as becomes evident in the following passage from the policy document (ibid.: 5):

> Since the youth are not only receptive to new ideas but also have the potential capacity for creativity and productivity, they can play a major role in all sectors of development. In order to translate their potential energies and capabilities into fruitful action, however, they need [a] favorable environment. If these conditions are not satisfied, they can immediately fall into the abyss of desperation, neglect everything and can become passive observers of the activities undertaken in the society. Not only that, they will also be exposed to social evils.

Kelly (2001: 24) explains this as follows: »Discourses of youth at risk are framed by the idea that youth should be a transition from normal childhood to normal adulthood;« therefore, the policy seeks to regulate the behaviour of youth populations thought to be at risk of not attaining transition and falling into deviancy and delinquency. As such they are guided by often competing »humanistic and economic concerns« (ibid.). This is also evident in the passage from the Ethiopian Youth Policy quoted above, which finds youth potentiality to be in jeopardy should it not be structured into productive behaviour. To remedy this problem, »the basic task of the policy is to change the existing objective conditions towards the full utilization of the potential capacity of youth for the country's development effort« (ibid.: 18). How, then, is the potential of youth to be unlocked? Perhaps surprisingly in light of the state-centred development model advocated by the government, the policy calls for a larger role of the private sector in job creation, and it advocates conditions that would allow youths to take on an entrepreneurial role in the country's economy and, thus, create employment for themselves. What is more, although the problem of youth unemployment in Ethiopia is acknowledged, the policy also postulates that the problem is aggravated by the prevalent societal belief that responsibility for solving the issue of unemployment lies with the government. As a solution to this problem the policy envisions the formation of an entrepreneurial youth. In this way responsibility for employment possibilities is shifted onto young people themselves and away from the government.

Such an image of an entrepreneurial and responsible youth also conforms to visions of youth put forth in the global development discourse advocated by supra-national organisations like the World Bank (Sukarieh and Tannock 2008) and the United Nations (Bersaglio, Enns and Kepe 2015). These organisations frame youth as ›assets‹ to be developed, and critical scholars argue that it is the incorporation into neoliberal market relations that is at heart of such projects even if this is couched in such buzzwords as ›empowerment‹ and claims of supporting youth agency (Sukarieh and Tannock 2008; Bersaglio, Enns and Kepe 2015). For so-called developing countries this means formulating approaches to youth development in terms that are consistent with these types of agenda, as this is a prerequisite for obtaining donors' support for youth-related programmes. However, Sukarieh and Tannock (2011: 688) remind us that »the mobilization of positive and negative images of youth is always linked to particular political projects and visions in the context of changing social and economic structures.« Thus, a report for the International Labour Organisation notes that Ethiopian youth policy does not »focus entirely on the development and welfare of the youth« but instead on the »context of the interest of the country as a whole« (Denu, Tekeste and Van der Deijl 2005). By drawing on a rhetoric of risk and potential, Ethiopian youth policy seeks to construct youth as a social category in ways that serve the developmental project of the ruling regime. Rather than the ›interest of the country as a whole‹, it is the hegemony of the developmental project that frames youth policy and politics vis-à-vis youth. As such the policy employs a dual vision of youth potential and risk in order to make youth responsible and entrepreneurial subjects.

### Youth Entrepreneurship Programmes

The promotion and implementation of youth-related development schemes accelerated in the aftermath of the 2005 elections; critically, many young people had been at the forefront of the protests that ensued (Abbink 2006). A Youth Development Programme was launched in 2007 with the support of UNICEF in order to provide entrepreneurship and other types of training through government-owned youth centres (MoFED and UNICEF 2012). The organisation of youths into economic cooperatives was pursued in tandem with the recruitment of young people into the political structures of the EPRDF. In 2009 the Youth League of the ruling party was formed (Gebremariam and Lule 2014), and observers noted that the party had before that already increased efforts to enrol university students into the party (Vaughan 2011).

It is against this background that Di Nunzio (2015) asserts that, politically, small and micro-enterprise schemes were deemed by the EPRDF to be a way to recapture the support of youths by allowing the incumbent party to assert itself as the force that was most able to provide them with economic opportunities. This rationality is closely linked with the ruling party's ideological commitment to development, as Di Nunzio further argues. It shaped an understanding that it had been largely a lack of employment opportunities which had led youths to take part in the protests of 2005. During the protests government discourse criminalised young protesters as ›dangerous vagrants‹ (*adegegna bozene*), and unemployment was seen as the main reason for their ›criminal behaviour‹ (Di Nunzio 2015). Tackling unemployment was deemed to be a vital tool in mobilising political support and suppressing dissent among the youth (ibid.). He goes on to point out that the solution to youth unemployment was not simply believed to lie in providing jobs for young people but in envisioning young people as entrepreneurs (ibid.: 1187). He maintains that the ideological underpinnings of the government shaped a particular understanding of entrepreneurship: not as a mainly individual venture as part of a liberal economy, but as a collective undertaking that served the development of the country as a whole.

This notwithstanding, I argue that it is precisely the liberal element that makes the discourse of entrepreneurship so attractive to the Ethiopian government. That is to say that by emphasising the need for attitudinal adjustment and individual responsibility in the target group, unemployment could be focused on at a subjective level – and thus outside the economic supra-structures ostensibly controlled by the party-state. In this I follow Bach (2011: 643), who argues that the party's ideology does not represent a ›static discourse‹ in strict opposition to market liberal policy but, instead, operates in a flexible manner that allows for the adaptation of market principles into the developmental project. The linking of an individual enterprise to the collective endeavour of development is one such example.

The sociologist Pat O'Malley (2000) has termed this type of transformation of societal risk into the scope of collective and individual subjects as ›new prudentialism‹. The ›prudent‹ enterprising subject engages in ›exercises of uncertainty‹ in order to generate surplus that makes the management of risk possible. In this way the self is obliged to responsibility as a moral agent and constructed as a calculative rational-choice actor. However such ›responsibilisation‹ strategies have been conceptualised mainly in the context of liberal individualism and the freedom of citizens to make a series of considered choices in various spheres (see Rose 1999; Lemke 2002). In the Ethiopian case it is state-led development, which is envisioned as a collective endeavour, that frames the responsibilisation of subjects to become self-enterprising market actors within a much narrower conception of personal freedom.

These examples serve to show how the ruling party employs Youth Development Programmes in order to foster political allegiance and closer links to young people across the country. In this context disengagement from the developmental agenda of the state is increasingly difficult for young people because it is the state that controls access to education, employment and other benefits. As Di Nunzio's (2014; 2015) work has shown, the formalisation of previously informal (small) business sectors has increased the government's reach into the lives of young people. In the next section I will look at programmes where the target group consists of those individuals with a higher education, for whom the state remains the main employer (Broussard and Tekleselassie 2012). The programmes discussed in this contribution appear to aim at changing this fact by promoting self-employment.

## Entrepreneurship discourse in Ethiopia through the lens of training programmes

Entrepreneurship education at institutions of higher education in Ethiopia is still in its infancy, and there is not yet a unified approach on how to integrate entrepreneurship into institutions' syllabi (Gerba 2012). However, there is an indication of strong political will to change this situation; efforts are underway to establish centres of excellence in entrepreneurship at the major Ethiopian universities.[4] Several entrepreneurship training programmes are currently supported by international organisations, and a host of international non-governmental organisations are similarly

---

4 | The six institutions where these centres are being established are: Addis Ababa University, Addis Ababa Science and Technology University, Adama Science and Technology University, Mekelle University, Bahir Dar University, and Hawassa University (Interview #2, 2014).

engaged in promoting entrepreneurship in Ethiopia, with youths and women as the main target groups.

In the following section, I concentrate on the work of the Entrepreneurship Development Center (EDC) and the discursive framing of entrepreneurship by government officials as well as the staff of the centre. Furthermore, I will briefly discuss the work of international NGOs that run long-term training programmes in entrepreneurship for youth.

## The Entrepreneurship Development Center (EDC): A governmental institution?

The EDC is officially designated as a quasi-governmental entity which operates under direction of the Ethiopian Ministry of Urban Development, Housing and Construction (MoUDHCo) and was established in the framework of the Entrepreneurship Development Program (EDP) in early 2013. It receives technical and financial support from the United Nations Development Program (UNDP) and the government of Canada (UNDP 2014). Its mandate is to develop »best practices and [pilot] promising initiatives of entrepreneurship development« (EDP 2014) in order to support the goals and visions of the Growth and Transformation Plan (GTP) of the Ethiopian government. The GTP is a five-year poverty-reduction and development plan that aims to transform Ethiopia into a middle-income country by 2025. It explicitly acknowledges the issue of youth unemployment and places an emphasis on Micro and Small Enterprises (MSE) as a means of job creation (MoFED 2010).

The EDC runs short-term, six-day intensive Entrepreneurship Training Workshops (ETWs) with the purpose to »develop entrepreneurial mindsets and behaviors in participants« (EDP 2014). The methodology used in the training is based on the work of the late psychologist David McClelland (1961), who proposed that »everyone has an inner motivation to improve«. Through a process of self-assessment participants are asked to identify personal opportunities and to set personal goals. The training materials are developed by the UNDP as part of a standardised programme, which means that their content cannot be modified other than through translation into local languages and the introduction of contextualised examples.[5] In addition to this it provides a Business Development Service, which provides a more long-term form of support through different advisory mechanisms. Furthermore, because the EDC is mandated to encourage youth and female entrepreneurship, it offers so-called ›customised workshops‹ specifically for those target groups.

The ways in which the programme of the EDC frames entrepreneurship in relation to young people as well as the issue of unemployment will now be the focus of my discussion, and I shall explore two specific issues: first, how this shifts the moral responsibility for economic insecurity onto young graduates themselves, and second, how this recasts uncertainty in a more positive way by treating it as a business-related risk.

## Framing entrepreneurship

On the occasion of the opening of the EDC in February 2013, the current prime minister of Ethiopia Hailemariam Desalegn, who gave the keynote speech, not only framed the mandate of the EDC in terms of supporting the goals of the GTP. He also pointed to the problematic nature of youth unemployment (Hailemariam 2013; emphasis added):

With the number of graduates growing by leaps and bounds and the number of the youth population bulging every year, dependable ways of creating massive employment opportunities is an imperative. *As much as our huge youth population can be a source of strength and growth, it could also be a source of vulnerability and social tension* unless we are in a position to offer job opportunities that can absorb this huge chunk of our population.

Similarly to the Ethiopian Youth Policy outlined above, youths here are framed in a dual manner, as both a potential asset and a possible liability. Regarding the aims and goals of the EDC, the prime minister underscored that (ibid.; emphasis added):

---

**5 |** Based on personal observations, it appears as though workshop materials are only partly translated; much of the translation is done ad hoc by the trainers, which demands great effort on their part. Further examples given are often taken from outside of an Ethiopian context. These factors may reduce workshop participants' comprehension of the programme.

This project will not be confined to providing training entrepreneurship skills important as that may be. *It should strive towards bringing about attitudinal change in our society.* Without a change in the attitude of the society and the development of social capital sustaining our growth spiral is almost impossible.

The prime minister's statement shows that entrepreneurship training is not just meant to influence those who directly participate in it, but that the programme is expected to achieve an attitudinal transformation for society in general and to contribute to national economic growth. On the same occasion other government officials further emphasised that young graduates should themselves create jobs for others through entrepreneurial start-ups rather than remaining ›job-seekers‹ and seeing the government as the main generator of employment (Haile 2013).

In the interviews that I conducted in 2014, I repeatedly encountered this sentiment: »They should not look for government employment,« (Interview #1, 2014) one employee of the Federal Agency for Micro and Small Enterprise Development told me; another official framed young graduates as being too passive when he explained that »they sit and wait for [the] government to give [them] employment« (Interview #2, 2014).

These types of statements need to be contextualised. Government employment is regarded as a preferred choice for university graduates, followed by employment in white-collar jobs in the private and non-governmental sector (Broussard and Tekleselassie 2012). However the massive growth of the Ethiopian education system, particularly the higher education sector, makes the absorption of graduates by these sectors increasingly difficult. Starting in the early 2000s, the Ethiopian government in collaboration with external donors has invested heavily into the expansion of higher education (Negash 2006). In 1999 the country only had two public universities; by 2014 this number had increased to 32 universities under the administration of the Ministry of Education (Ministry of Education 2015). In the same period the enrolment of full-time undergraduates at public universities grew from almost 20,000 in 1999 to nearly 400,000 in 2014 (ibid.). This means that nearly 80,000 full-time students graduated from the universities with a Bachelor's degree in 2014 alone. While a small percentage of graduates continue their education in graduate programmes, the majority seek employment opportunities in the labour market. Studies on youth unemployment have shown that in the last decade the percentage of university graduates who are without employment has steadily increased (Broussard and Tekleselassie 2012). High unemployment rates are especially pronounced for urban youth, amounting to 28 per cent for male and nearly 19 per cent for female university graduates in 2011 (ibid.).

Case studies conducted by anthropologists (Mains 2011) and sociologists (Serneels 2007) have pointed out that unemployment in Ethiopia might not only be related to the unavailability of jobs but also to cultural notions connected with the social status of certain kinds of work. They suggest that especially young people with a higher educational background seem to prefer ›queuing‹ for employment opportunities in the public sector as opposed to private sector employment or informal jobs. Employment statistics indeed show that most graduates with a higher form of education are employed in the public sector, and that the likelihood of self-employment decreases sharply the higher their educational status is. The same is true for private-sector employment (Broussard and Tekleselassie 2012). These statistics also point to a steady decrease over the course of the last decade of people with a higher educational background in self-employed occupations.

My interlocutors also emphasised cultural notions as a reason for why the general motivation to become an entrepreneur is not high. When I asked about the major challenges of starting one's own business, a training manager replied:

When you ask people out there to tell you the major challenges that they face to set up their own enterprise, they mention financial problem, seed money, things like that. *But from my observation [...] the major problem is [the] failure to have the right attitude about entrepreneurship.* The culture in which we grew up doesn't motivate people to become entrepreneurs. [...] We value governmental jobs, or being employed [...]. So this culture is impeding many entrepreneurs, especially young people to think entrepreneurially. So for me the main challenge is failure to have the right attitude. (Interview #3, 2014; emphasis added.)

Here we can see that a structural problem to starting a business, such as access to finance, is set aside in order to emphasise cultural and attitudinal factors that are believed to explain the lack of motivation to become an entrepreneur. How, then, are young people motivated to consider entrepreneurship? In a two-day orientation workshop offered to university students, the benefits of entrepreneurship are presented in the following way, as my interview partner further elaborated:

> The whole intention of this training is to give them orientation [...] about the advantages that they are going to get out of entrepreneurship. *And we also try to emphasise that working for other institutions as an employee is staying in bondage, and we try to emphasise that they have to break this bondage and become free* and think for themselves [rather] than work for others and become [...] employees [...]. (Interview #3, 2014; emphasis added.)

In order to make entrepreneurship attractive to university students, it is framed as a liberating occupational choice that can free the individual subject from the ›bondage‹ of employment. Foucault's concept of ›governmentality‹ serves as an appropriate tool for interpretation here. According to Lemke (2002: 53) it allows us to understand that power relations are not necessarily marked by fewer choices available to the individual but by a form of responsibilisation that compels subjects into making ›free decisions‹. Thus, social risks such as unemployment can be shifted into the domain of ›self-care‹ (ibid.: 59). In a set of interviews I conducted with participants of entrepreneurship programmes, ›freedom‹ was mentioned repeatedly as a motivation for pursuing self-employment; in other words, the promise of one day being one's own boss seemed to resonate with the target group, especially those who already had some experience with employment. It appears that in a society with strong hierarchical boundaries, entrepreneurship promises not merely economic success but personal freedoms, too. In this way entrepreneurship not only plays to the aspirations of young people but also structures their desire for freedom in terms of becoming a successful market actor.

## Producing the enterprising self

In the work of international NGOs (INGOs) operating in Ethiopia that run long-term mentoring and training programmes, a focus on the development of enterprising behaviour seems especially pronounced. I now take a closer look at two programmes of this type that specifically focus on young people with a higher educational background. I am interested here in the degree to which notions of entrepreneurship are articulated in terms that differ from, or are similar to, those used in the programme described above.

When the director of such a training programme outlined its purpose, he highlighted that the programme was not merely teaching skills but also addressing behavioural matters:

> This training focuses on attitudinal change, [...] how does a person see himself or herself? Where is the place of that person in the society, in the community, and so, what are the kind of assets that the people think they have and they could have? You know, what is the kind of network that they have, and [that] they could have? [...] So it's broadening their mindset, broadening their understanding of their context, broadening their self-awareness [...] and then complementing that with specific skills about running businesses. (Interview #4, 2014.)

Here, too, young people are encouraged to start their own businesses and are urged to look beyond structural obstructions. They are encouraged to rely on their own resourcefulness and to activate their social network, that is, to look for business opportunities in their direct surroundings and to find financial support among relatives and within their immediate social network. It is also implied that the training increases participants' self-awareness.

Similarly, a blog post about a mentoring programme focused on female university students in Addis Ababa highlights how participants learned to unfold their ›unexploited‹ potential (CCL 2015):

> Through [the programme, the organisation] was able to produce a promising new batch of female entrepreneurial leaders who are confident on the things they like to do in their lives rather than struggling with what they have to do. Evaluating the program showed that most of the participants developed a new skill set, opened up to new perspectives about their chances in life and ways of impacting their society. Students learned that limited resources do not necessarily imply limited business and entrepreneurial opportunities. Obviously, the program helped participants to think and act beyond their social and economical [sic] boundaries.

By employing a terminology of capitalist manufacturing, the author reveals the belief that it is possible to produce young people with an entrepreneurial identity through their socialisation into a particular type of behaviour. Furthermore, a discourse centred on potential, self-reflection and responsibility for one's own development seems to emphasise that it is only the constant optimisation of oneself and a commitment to the logics of the market that can bring about progress in life. Consequently we have to ask what it means to ›act beyond social and economic boundaries‹. Does this mean that the uncertainty and anxieties of young people can simply be overcome through the correct amount of confidence and self-determination? According to the diverse arguments cited above, their chances of having an impact on society are limited only by their own perceptions and attitudes.

## Conclusion

In this chapter I have outlined central aspects of entrepreneurship promotion and training as they have been addressed in scholarly literature. The examples that I have discussed show that entrepreneurship training programmes in Ethiopia – both those closely linked to the government as well as those run by INGOs – are based on similar understandings of the ›producibility‹ of enterprising identities among young people. This notion can be linked to the general aims of entrepreneurship education to enhance particular attitudes towards risks and opportunities in their target groups. To a certain extent, then, this discourse is informed by globally circulating ideas on how entrepreneurship can bring about growth and create employment opportunities.

However, as I have shown with reference to the relevant literature and in my analysis of official discourse, the Ethiopian party-state is able to shape these programmes in a way that allows it to frame local problems in the context of its own developmental and political agenda. In the specific case of Ethiopia, discourse on entrepreneurship serves to frame a politics of responsibilisation vis-à-vis the country's youth. Therefore, these programmes are guided by the state's ambition to create entrepreneurial subjects in line with the government's developmental ideology.

To conclude, entrepreneurship discourse forms the context of action in which young people engage with uncertain futures in two ways. First, it emphasises the necessity of an attitudinal change in the target group, thereby transforming the largely structural problem of unemployment into a question of individual mentality and shifting the moral responsibility for economic insecurity away from the state and onto young graduates.

Second, the uncertainties of starting a business are shown in a more positive light by pointing to the ›liberating‹ aspects of entrepreneurship.

The ›mind-shift‹ required from programme participants not only serves to eliminate economic insecurity but also to devise a managerial approach to such economic contingency, in the sense of being able to navigate market volatility so as to produce jobs and growth in Ethiopia. Further questions of why self-employment seems so unattractive to graduates of higher education in Ethiopia are pushed to the background. While they are not completely negated, the uncertainties and risk of failure are downplayed; and success becomes a matter of having the right attitude. The structural problems of access to finance, bureaucratic hurdles and the fact that the needs of industry are not matched by the education system are toned down.

Beyond this, the implication of international agencies in the developmental agenda of the Ethiopian government by way of monetary and ›knowledge aid‹ has yet to be scrutinised. It seems that the ›youth question‹ is addressed by these very different actors in a similar fashion: by prescribing the market as the only possible answer to economic uncertainty. Consequently, further research should take a closer look at the consequences of such an entanglement, both in the (re-)formulation of entrepreneurship training in general, and the concrete content of such instruction in particular.

## Interviews

(All interviews have been anonymised to protect the identity of the interviewees.)

Interview #1, 6 March, 2014; Addis Ababa, Ethiopia.
Interview #2, 11 March, 2014; Addis Ababa, Ethiopia.
Interview #3, 4 December, 2014; Addis Ababa, Ethiopia.
Interview #4, 25 November, 2014; Addis Ababa, Ethiopia.

## Bibliography

(All Ethiopian officials are identified by their first name because identification by surname is not common in Ethiopia.)

Aalen, Lovise, Kjetil Tronvoll. 2009. »The End of Democracy? Curtailing Political and Civil Rights in Ethiopia.« *Review of African Political Economy* 36(120): 193–207.

Abbink, Jon. 2006. »Discomfiture of Democracy? The 2005 Election Crisis in Ethiopia and Its Aftermath.« *African Affairs* 105(419): 173–199.

—. 2011. »Ethnic-Based Federalism and Ethnicity in Ethiopia: Reassessing the Experiment after 20 Years.« *Journal of Eastern African Studies* 5(4): 596–618.

Amit, Raphael, Lawrence Glosten, Eitan Muller. 1993. »Challenges to Theory Development in Entrepreneurship Research.« *Journal of Management Studies* 30(5): 815–834.

Bach, Jean-Nicolas. 2011. »Abyotawi Democracy: Neither Revolutionary nor Democratic, a Critical Review of EPRDF's Conception of Revolutionary Democracy in Post-1991 Ethiopia.« *Journal of Eastern African Studies* 5(4): 641–663.

Berglund, Karin. 2013. »Fighting against All Odds: Entrepreneurship Education as Employability Training.« *Ephemera* 13(4): 717–735.

Bersaglio, Brock, Charis Enns, Thembela Kepe. 2015. »Youth under Construction: The United Nations' Representations of Youth in the Global Conversation on the Post-2015 Development Agenda.« *Canadian Journal of Development Studies / Revue Canadienne D'études Du Développement* 36(1): 57–71.

Binswanger, Hans Christoph. 2006. *Die Wachstumsspirale: Geld, Energie und Imagination in der Dynamik des Marktprozesse*. Marburg: Metropolis.

Blum, Douglas W. 2007. *National Identity and Globalization: Youth, State, and Society in Post-Soviet Eurasia*. Cambridge: Cambridge University Press.

Bromber, Katrin, Paolo Gaibazzi, Franziska Roy, Abdoulaye Sounaye, Julian Tadesse. 2015. »›The Possibilities Are Endless‹: Progress and the Taming of Contingency.« *Zentrum Moderner Orient*, Programatic Texts no.9.

Broussard, Nzinga, Tsegay Gebrekidan Tekleselassie. 2012. »Youth Unemployment: Ethiopia Country Study.« *International Growth Centre*, Working Paper no.12.

Brown, Phillip, Anthony Hesketh, Sara Wiliams. 2003. »Employability in a Knowledge-Driven Economy.« *Journal of Education and Work* 16(2): 107–126.

Burchell, Graham. 1993. »Liberal Government and Techniques of the Self.« *Economy and Society* 22(3): 267–282.

Cantillon, Richard. 2015. *Richard Cantillon's Essay on the Nature of Trade in General: A Variorum Edition*. London: Routledge.

CCL. 2015. »New Ways for Women Empowerment: Social Innovation in Ethiopia|Leadership Beyond Boundaries.« *Leadership Beyond Boundaries – An Initiative of Center for Creative Leadership*. Retrieved 13 March, 2016. [http://leadbeyond.org/2013/05/15/new-ways-for-women-empowerment-social-innovation-in-ethiopia]

Chinigò, Davide, Emanuele Fantini. 2015. »Thermidor in Ethiopia? Agrarian Transformations between Economic Liberalization and the Developmental State.« *EchoGéo* 31 (April).

Denu, Berhanu, Abraham Tekeste, Hannah Van der Deijl. 2005. *Characteristics and Determinants of Youth Unemployment, Underemployment and Inadequate Employment in Ethiopia*. Geneva: International Labour Office.

Di Nunzio, Marco. 2014. »›Do Not Cross the Red Line‹: The 2010 General Elections, Dissent, and Political Mobilization in Urban Ethiopia.« *African Affairs* 113(452): 409–430.

—. 2015. »What Is the Alternative? Youth, Entrepreneurship and the Developmental State in Urban Ethiopia.« *Development and Change* 46(5): 1179–1200.

EDP. 2014. »Entrepreneurship Development Centre – Fact Sheet.« *Entrepreneurship Development Centre*. Retrieved 25 March, 2016. [http://www.edcethiopia.org/images/pdf/EDC_Fact_Sheet-March_25_2014.pdf]

Fantini, Emanuele. 2013. »Developmental State, Economic Transformation and Social Diversification in Ethiopia.« *ISPI Analysis* 163(March). Retrieved 25 March, 2016. [http://www.ispionline.it/sites/default/files/pubblicazioni/analysis_163_2013.pdf]

Fayolle, Alain. 2007. *Handbook of Research in Entrepreneurship Education. 1. A General Perspective*. Cheltenham: Elgar.

Ferguson, James. 2010. »The Uses of Neoliberalism.« *Antipode* 41(s1): 166–184.

Foucault, Michel. 2000. *Power*. Edited by James D Faubion. New York: New Press.

Gartner, William B. 1988. »Who Is the Entrepreneur? Is the Wrong Question.« *American Journal of Small Business* 12(4): 11–32.

Gebremariam, Eyob Balcha, Hallelujah Lule. 2014. »Towards Youthful, Useful Youth Policy.« *Addis Fortune* 15(759). Retrieved 16 November, 2016. [http://addisfortune.net/columns/towards-youthful-useful-youth-policy]

Gerba, Dugassa Tessema. 2012. »The Context of Entrepreneurship Education in Ethiopian Universities.« *Management Research Review* 35(3/4): 225–244.

Hagmann, Tobias, Jon Abbink. 2011. »Twenty Years of Revolutionary Democratic Ethiopia, 1991 to 2011.« *Journal of Eastern African Studies* 5(4): 579–595.

Haile, Mekuria. 2013. »Speech – Minister Mekuria Haile – Launch of Ethiopia's Entrepreneurship Development Programme, UNDP.« Ministry of Urban Development and Construction, Addis Ababa, Ethiopia, 19 February. Retrieved 13 March, 2016. [http://www.undp.org/content/ethiopia/en/home/presscenter/speeches/2013/02/19/minister-mekuria-haile-launch-of-ethiopia-s-entrepreneurship-development-programme]

Hailemariam, Desalegn. 2013. »Launch of Ethiopia's Entrepreneurship Development Programme.« Keynote Address by Ethiopian Prime Minister, Addis Ababa, 19 February. Retrieved 13 March, 2016. [http://www.undp.org/content/ethiopia/en/home/presscenter/speeches/2013/02/19/ethiopia-prime-minister-hailemariam-desalegn-s-keynote-address-launch-of-ethiopia-s-entrepreneurship-development-programme.html]

Hansson, Stina. 2014. »Analysing Responsibilisation in the Context of Development Cooperation.« In *Studying the Agency of Being Governed: Methodological Reflections*, edited by Stina Hansson, Sofie Hellberg, and Maria Stern. London and New York: Routledge. 130–149.

Holmgren, Carina, Jorgen From. 2008. »Taylorism of the Mind: Entrepreneurship Education from a Perspective of Educational Research.« *European Educational Research Journal* 4(4): 382–390.

Human Rights Watch. 2010. »›One Hundred Ways of Putting Pressure‹ – Violations of Freedom of Expression and Association in Ethiopia.« New York: Human Rights Watch. Retrieved 13 March, 2016. [https://www.hrw.org/report/2010/03/24/one-hundred-ways-putting-pressure/violations-freedom-expression-and-association]

Kelly, Peter. 2001. »Youth at Risk: Processes of Individualisation and Responsibilisation in the Risk Society.« *Discourse: Studies in the Cultural Politics of Education* 22(1): 23–33.

Lefort, René. 2012. »Free Market Economy, ›Developmental State‹ and Party-State Hegemony in Ethiopia: The Case of the ›Model Farmers‹. *The Journal of Modern African Studies* 50(4): 681–706.

Lemke, Thomas. 2002. »Foucault, Governmentality, and Critique.« *Rethinking Marxism* 14(3): 49–64.

Lingelbach, David C., De La Vina, Lynda, Paul Asel. 2005. »What's Distinctive about Growth-Oriented Entrepreneurship in Developing Countries?« SSRN Scholarly Paper ID 742605. Rochester, NY: Social Science Research Network. Retrieved 13 March, 2016. [http://papers.ssrn.com/abstract=742605]

Mahieu, Ron. 2006. »Agents of Change and Policies of Scale: A Policy Study of Entrepreneurship and Enterprise in Education.« PhD dissertation, University of Umeå.

Mains, Daniel. 2011. »Cynicism and Hope: Urban Youth and Relations of Power During the 2005 Ethiopian Elections.« In *Contested Power in Ethiopia: Traditional Authorities and Multi-Party Elections*, edited by Kjetil Tronvoll and Tobias Hagmann. Leiden: Brill. 137–164.

McClelland, David C. 1961. *The Achieving Society*. New York: Free Press.

Meles, Zenawi. 2012. »States and Markets: Neoliberal Limitations and the Case for a Developmental State.« In *Good Growth and Governance in Africa: Rethinking Development Strategies*, edited by Joseph Stiglitz et al. New York: Columbia University. 140–174.

Miettinen, A. 2003. »Entrepreneurship as an Ability Game: Observations from Children's and Adolescent's Microstoria.« In *IntEnt2002: Internationalizing Entrepreneurship Education and Training – Proceedings of the IntEnt-Conference Johore Bahru, Malaysia, July 8-10, 2002*, edited by Heinz Klandt and Ahmad Zaki Abu Bakar. Lohmar: Eul.

Ministry of Education. 2015. »Education Statistics National Abstract 2013-14.« Addis Ababa, Ethiopia: Federal Democratic Republic of Ethiopia. Retrieved 13 March, 2016. [http://www.moe.gov.et/English/

Information/Documents/Education%20Statistics%20Annual%20 Abstract%202006E.C%20(2013-2014%20G.C).pdf]

Ministry of Youth, Sports and Culture. 2004. »Federal Democratic Republic of Ethiopia – National Youth Policy.« Addis Ababa. Retrieved 13 March, 2016. [http://www.youthpolicy.org/national/Ethiopia_2004_National_Youth_Policy.pdf]

MoFED. 2010. *Growth and Transformation Plan (2010/11-2014/15)*. Vol. I. Addis Ababa, Ethiopia: Ministry of Finance and Economic Development (MoFED).

MoFED, and UNICEF. 2012. »Evaluation of the UNICEF/MOWCYA Adolescent/Youth Development Programme in Ethiopia (2007-2011).« Ministry of Finance and Economic Development and UNICEF in Ethiopia. Retrieved 13 March, 2016. [http://www.unicef.org/evaluation/files/Ethiopia_2012-049_Adolescent_Development_Final_Report.pdf]

Molla, Tebeje. 2013. »Knowledge Aid as Instrument of Regulation: World Bank's Non-Lending Higher Education Support for Ethiopia.« *Comparative Education* 50(2): 229–248.

Neamin, Ashenafi. 2015. »Ethiopian Election | Beyene Petros Sour about the Electoral Process.« *The Reporter*. May 30. Retrieved 13 March, 2016. http://hornaffairs.com/en/2015/06/01/ethiopian-election-beyene-petros-sour-about-the-electoral-process/.

Negash, Tekeste. 2006. *Education in Ethiopia: From Crisis to the Brink of Collapse*. Discussion Paper 33. Uppsala: Nordiska Afrikainstitutet.

Ogbor, John O. 2000. »Mythicizing and Reification in Entrepreneurial Discourse: Ideology-Critique of Entrepreneurial Studies.« *Journal of Management Studies* 37(5): 605–635.

O'Malley, Pat. 1996. »Risk and Responsibility.« In *Foucault and Political Reason: Liberalism, Neo-Liberalism, and Rationalities of Government*, edited by Andrew Barry, Thomas Osborne, and Nikolas S Rose. Chicago: University of Chicago Press. 189–207.

—. 2000. »Uncertain Subjects: Risks, Liberalism and Contract.« *Economy and Society* 29(4): 460–484.

Ong, Aihwa. 2006. *Neoliberalism as Exception: Mutations in Citizenship and Sovereignty*. Duke University Press.

Peters, Michael A. 2016. »From State Responsibility for Education and Welfare to Self-Responsibilisation in the Marke.« *Discourse: Studies in the Cultural Politics of Education* (April).

Robb, Alicia, Alexandria Valerio, Brent Parton (eds). 2014. *Entrepreneurship Education and Training: Insights from Ghana, Kenya, and Mozambique.* The World Bank. Retrieved 13 March, 2016. [http://elibrary.worldbank.org/doi/book/10.1596/978-1-4648-0278-2]

Rose, Nikolas S. 1999. *Powers of Freedom: Reframing Political Thought.* Cambridge: Cambridge University Press.

Schumpeter, Joseph A. 2006 [1912]. *Theorie der wirtschaftlichen Entwicklung.* Berlin: Duncker & Humblot.

Serneels, Pieter. 2007. »The Nature of Unemployment among Young Men in Urban Ethiopia.« *Review of Development Economics* 11(1): 170–186.

Shamir, Ronen. 2008. »The Age of Responsibilization: On Market-Embedded Morality.« *Economy and Society* 37(1): 1–19.

Shane, Scott A. 1997. »Who Is Publishing the Entrepreneurship Research?« *Journal of Management* 23(1): 83–95.

Sukarieh, Mayssoun. 2012. »From Terrorists to Revolutionaries: The Emergence of ›Youth‹ in the Arab World and the Discourse of Globalization.« *Interface* 4(2): 424–437.

Sukarieh, Mayssoun, Stuart Tannock. 2008. »In the Best Interests of Youth or Neoliberalism? The World Bank and the New Global Youth Empowerment Project.« *Journal of Youth Studies* 11(3): 301–312.

—. 2011. »The Positivity Imperative: A Critical Look at the ›New‹ Youth Development Movement.« *Journal of Youth Studies* 14(6): 675–691.

Trnka, Susanna, Catherine Trundle. 2014. »Competing Responsibilities: Moving Beyond Neoliberal Responsibilisation.« *Anthropological Forum* 24(2): 136–153.

UNDP. 2004. »Unleashing Entrepreneurship: Making Business Work for the Poor.« Report to the Secretary-General of the United Nations. Commission on the Private Sector and Development. United Nations Development Programme.

—. 2013. »Ethiopia Launches New Entrepreneurship Development Programme | UNDP.« *United Nations Development Programme.* Retrieved 13 March, 2016. [http://www.undp.org/content/ethiopia/en/home/ourwork/povertyreduction/news/ethiopia-launches-new-entrepreneurship-programme-1]

—. 2014. »Canada Provides 5.8 Million USD in Grant to Support Ethiopia's Women Entrepreneurs.« *United Nations Development Program in Ethiopia.* April 10. Retrieved 13 March, 2016. [http://www.et.undp.org/content/ethiopia/en/home/presscenter/pressreleases/2014/04/10/

canada-provides-over-5-8-million-usd-in-grant-to-support-ethiopia-s-women-entrepreneurs.html]

Vaughan, Sarah. 2011. »Revolutionary Democratic State-Building: Party, State and People in the EPRDF's Ethiopia.« *Journal of Eastern African Studies* 5(4): 619–640.

Vaughan, Sarah, Mesfin Gebremichael. 2011. »Rethinking Business and Politics in Ethiopia: The Role of EFFORT, the Endowment Fund for the Rehabilitation of Tigray.« *Africa Power and Politics Research Report* 02. Retrieved 13 March, 2016. [http://research.dfid.gov.uk/r4d/PDF/Outputs/APPP/20110822-appp-rr02-rethinking-business-politics-in-ethiopia-by-sarah-vaughan-mesfin-gebremichael-august-2011.pdf]

Volkmann, Christine, K. E. Wilson, S. Mariotti, D. Rabuzzi, S. Vyakarnam, A. Sepulveda. 2009. »Educating the Next Wave of Entrepreneurs: Unlocking Entrepreneurial Capabilities to Meet the Global Challenges of the 21st Century.« A Report of the Global Education Initiative. Geneva: World Economic Forum.

World Bank. 2012. »World Bank Provides Funding to Unleash the Economic Potential of Ethiopian Women Entrepreneurs.« May 24. Retrieved 13 March, 2016. [http://www.worldbank.org/en/news/press-release/2012/05/24/world-bank-provides-funding-to-unleash-the-economic-potential-of-ethiopian-women-entrepreneurs]

World Economic Forum. 2009. »Educating the Next Wave of Entrepreneurs: Unlocking Entrepreneurial Capabilities to Meet the Global Challenges of the 21st Century.« A Report of the Global Education Initiative. Geneva: World Economic Forum.

# 8 Epilogue

Uncertainty and Elusive Futures

*Elísio Macamo*

## INTRODUCTION

Social life is really rather fascinating. There is much that happens in it which we take for granted. Thus, we go to bed and know that we will wake up the next morning. We rise and are more or less confident that the day ahead will be more or less like all other days. Of course, special events impose limitations on this: when we go to a job interview, we do not know if we will get the job. But even in this case, if we have met some of the conditions that we should fulfil in order to qualify for the job, we can still be reasonably confident that, all things being equal, we will get the job. This applies to many more things: being successful in courtship, getting her to say ›yes‹ to our marriage proposal or getting him to propose; doing well in exams; being invited to attend a conference. It also applies to life plans. All things being equal, if we take up studies, work hard, get the right grades and write the right kind of job application, we shall eventually get the job that will help us secure our livelihood and progress through the course of life from childhood and youth into adulthood and old age.

The problem lies in the caveat »all things being equal«. For all things to be equal we would need degrees of control over society, its institutions as well as, at least up to a certain point, nature which are not available to us, not even in totalitarian societies. All that we have to live by is the expectation that things might turn out well, all things being equal.... This raises a problem for social analysis. If social life resists the analysis that would yield the types of insight needed by individuals in order to formulate attainable goals, then of what use is social analysis? Who needs this kind of social analysis?

The purpose of this chapter is to discuss the theoretical and analytical issues raised by these questions. In order to do so, I start by offering an account of social life which seeks to show that the typical view of the nature of »the object« of the social sciences may be flawed and, for that reason, inadequate to help researchers frame their questions when they deal with subjects entailing a future temporal dimension. I offer a case in which I suggest that the notion of »uncertainty« provides a useful summary of this methodological predicament. Following this, I suggest that looking at social life from a perspective which focuses attention on the social situation may be a useful way of addressing these methodological challenges. The issues I raise in this chapter, therefore, draw implications from the research project on young graduates' career paths which provides the background for this volume.

As can easily be seen from these initial thoughts, the most fascinating aspect about social life is the extent to which our participation in it is largely determined by what we can take for granted and what we cannot. This insight was made relevant to sociology by the introduction of a phenomenological perspective into the sociology of knowledge (Berger and Luckmann 1991). The distinction between the problematic and non-problematic has made it clear that much social life consists in individuals translating what is unfamiliar to them into that which is familiar. In other words, they integrate relevant things happening in their everyday lives into that which they take for granted.

This insight suggests a distinction in social life between social actors who are optimists and those who are pessimists. Optimists are individuals who take everything for granted. Put differently, they assume that the next day will be the same as all the other days. These are the people who assume that, all things being equal, the outcomes of any situation will be the ones we expect, or for which we hope. For example, if today one woke up and went about one's daily chores without any kind of disruption, then the same will happen the next day. Everyday life in this case is entirely unproblematic and characterised largely by routine actions. Pessimists, by contrast, are those who cannot take social life for granted. These are the people who assume that what happens today does not allow us to assume that the next day will be the same.

In fact, in one case, i.e. in the case of the optimists, the assumption is that we live in a well-ordered social world which rewards everyone who does the right thing. Incidentally, this is the most typical fallacy of development thinking. The development industry in Africa, for example, entertains the belief that development as an outcome can be achieved by all those who do the right thing: to value and practice democracy, to be transparent and fight corruption, to care for the poor and the environment, etc. Conversely, therefore, where there is no development, it is because we are not doing the right thing. The fallacy is based on the (false) assumption that the world is fair and, therefore, that it rewards those who do the right thing. This is of course an inaccurate description of how development occurs. This is not to suggest that it is wrong to be an optimist; and such a conclusion is not warranted. Rather, it is to suggest that the assumption of a well-ordered world may not prepare us sufficiently well to all the things that happen in the social world and have the potential to undermine our plans. Research in the narrower field of risk sociology has shown with some degree of success that the harder we try to have the social world under our control, the more normal »breakdowns« become, that is, the likelier it is that their occurrence will become a function of the social system.[1]

In the other case, i.e. in the case of the pessimists, the assumption is that things in life are skewed against us such that positive outcomes are unlikely. An analogy with the African continent may be helpful in clarifying this point. Some African scholars and intellectuals (but, of course, this is not limited to these two groups) like to think, for instance, that development is not possible because the world is structurally biased against the African continent. The argument here is that no matter what Africans do, there is no way in which Africa can be successful as long as it is not in the interest of the neo-liberal forces that run the world. This, again, is an inaccurate representation of the world. There is nothing wrong with acknowledging the structural biases against the African continent. These biases explain why achieving certain outcomes is difficult, rather than why it is impossible.

The problem with optimists and pessimists is that they force us to focus overly on outcomes. By doing this we run the risk of either being normative in our approaches or of failing to consider alternative explanations for phenomena. Normativity arises when we judge social life based on desirable outcomes. While this is a perfectly legitimate attitude to take as a social actor, it is a highly problematic approach for

---

1 | Charles Perrow (1999) has made the best case for this view based on his research on technological disasters.

social researchers. A researcher desires to understand a situation and, if possible, to explain it, but not necessarily to make it happen. The problem with normativity is that it may mislead researchers into only searching for those things which will reassure them in their assumptions. One does not study market interactions at a sprawling informal market in an African city in order to help buyers achieve the best possible price. Rather, one studies them in order to understand how buying and selling occur. In contrast to this, the failure to consider alternative explanations comes from conceptualising the social world like an input/output machine. Again, an individual's success in securing a good price for a market item may be due to their expert bargaining skills, as well as to the vendor's desperate need to sell something that day.

There is, therefore, something about social life which makes it rather intractable from a methodological point of view. Two ways of approaching social life which are likely to yield poor results have to do, on the one hand, with the tendency to privilege outcomes over processes and, on the other hand, with how analysis is underdetermined by the normative expectations researchers bring to bear on them. These approaches appear to be the result of an unsatisfactory way of conceptualising social life – one which fails to give adequate weight to the uncertainty underlying it.

## SOCIAL SITUATIONS AND UNCERTAINTY

The opposition between optimists and pessimists can aid us to think through the subject of this volume. Both positions draw our attention to a very important aspect of social life: the idea that social situations consist of several parts, all of which come together in ways that are decisive for the outcomes.[2] These parts are essentially threefold. The first is what, for

---

2 | I derive the idea of »social situations« from the work of Randall Collins (2004). He explains its role in interaction ritual theory in the following relevant manner: »A theory of interaction ritual (IR) and interaction ritual chains is above all a theory of situations. It is a theory of momentary encounters among human bodies charged up with emotions and consciousness because they have gone through chains of previous encounters. What we mean by the social actor, the human individual, is a quasi-enduring, quasi-transient flux in time and space. Although we valorize and heroize this individual, we ought to recognize that this way of looking at things,

# 8 Epilogue  183

lack of a better word, I will call »interactional moments«; the second is the history that constituted them, i.e. social situations. The third, finally, consists of random factors. In other words, every time one approaches a social situation – buying something at a market, studying, fighting, etc. – one is typically addressing these three parts.

The »interactional moment« consists of the social actors (buyer and seller, ushers, bystanders), what they do (negotiating the price), and how they do it (in a friendly manner, in a clever way, etc.). Randall Collins' notion of interaction rituals, which he derived from the work of Durkheim and Erving Goffman, captures the essence of what is at stake in the description of such interactional moments (Collins 2004). The history that constituted buying/selling at a market consists of everything that makes this social situation recognisable as such (i.e. as being different from a robbery, for instance). Random factors can be a fire, a robbery or a riot of some sort, that is, anything that does not belong structurally to the situation, and which is not expected to happen yet can still happen. This understanding of social situations is crucial to the task which the authors of this volume set themselves: to seek ways in which they could grasp hold of the future in their work as researchers.

In essence, what I mean by interactional moments entails several elements: the expectations and motives of the social actors, the social positions of the social actors, the nature of the situation itself, i.e. whether it is a conflict or not, and several other minor elements. The history that constituted a social situation entails rules, norms and values as well as the degree to which the social situation has become routine. These bear directly on the structure of expectations and motives of social actors without, however, determining exactly how social actors will behave. Finally, random factors speak to the general idea that social situations happen within a larger social world from which social situations are insulated only up to a point.

This description reveals the problem made visible by the differences between optimists and the pessimists. Social situations are essentially like scripts, but unlike real scripts their authors have no control over the

---

this keyhole through which we peer at the universe, is the product of particular religious, political, and cultural trends of recent centuries. It is an ideology of how we regard it proper to think about ourselves and others, part of the folk idiom, not the most useful analytical starting point for microsociology« (Collins 2004: 3-4).

outcomes. In other words, acting consists in the ability to read the script properly and represent the situation adequately. However, both a proper reading of the script as well as an adequate representation of the situation are functions of the condition of the social actor herself or himself. This is the problem of contingency that has troubled sociology for a long time. Therefore, reading the script is to recognise the situation in one's own terms and to act it out according to the idea one has formed about the situation. This recognition and acting out may sometimes clash with the recognition and acting out of those with whom one interacts.

For this reason, the outcomes of social situations largely depend both on how stable the contexts are within which social action occurs, as well as on the ability of social actors to act accordingly. In other words, social situations have outcomes which are bad or good, but this does not depend on whether we do the right thing or whether situations are structurally skewed against us. The most basic feature of social situations is uncertainty; and this is a feature which social scientists in general and sociologists in particular have not been very good at accounting for. Uncertainty is at the heart of the career paths of young people in Africa. It expresses itself in the most pressing way when present-day action is expected to yield future outcomes.

In the history of sociology there have been essentially two ways of accounting for uncertainty. One – the traditional way – consisted in assuming the contingent nature of social interaction, i.e. the inability to safely predict the outcome of social action. This drew from the assumption that the outcome can hardly be predictable since action depends on the expectations and interpretations that interacting individuals have of their interlocutor's actions. However, instead of using this inability as an indication of a challenge in the description of social phenomena, sociologists focused their attention on solving the problem for social actors.

This traditional way was informed by a major preoccupation with the so-called problem of order, i.e. how is social order possible? Not surprisingly, the answer to this question (provided mainly by functionalist sociology) was to assume that individuals can be socialised into behaving in certain, predictable ways. In other words, through the internalisation of norms and values individuals can behave in ways which render outcomes predictable. For instance in Mali, which is one of the research sites of the project that produced this volume, the relative and purported importance of respect for elders could be seen in this way until, of course, the youth rebelled and shattered any explanatory value that there ever was in such an account.³

The second way of accounting for uncertainty was introduced by the sociology of risk. Its focus was on our ability to know; that is, the sociology of risk made the assumption that for structural reasons having to do with modernity, and especially technological modernity, social life had become too complex for us to be able to reduce it to simple algorithms. In fact, the operative term became »risk«, not uncertainty, and the dominant idea was that individuals were overwhelmed by situations, experts could not be trusted, and randomness could become the norm rather than the exception. This is the background against which the late German sociologist Ulrich Beck spoke of modern society as »risk society« (Beck 1992; see also Beck, Giddens and Lash 1994; Stehr 2001; Lupton 1999).

The problem with this way of accounting for uncertainty is that it rules out many societies – i.e. so-called non-modern societies – and fails to acknowledge that there is little analytical value in sociological accounts which mistake a universal social phenomenon for a particular manifestation of a single culture with the aim of constructing difference (see Macamo 2017). This is akin to observing how negotiation skills are crucial for trading at an informal market and then concluding that this corresponds to the commercial nature of Malian society, for example, which it does not share with other societies. This is obviously wrong, and good social science must seek to identify the social phenomenon at work and focus its attention on it.

Another German sociologist, Niklas Luhmann, made an important correction to this by drawing a distinction between danger and risk (Luhmann 1993). He argued that danger is what happens to us, whereas risk is what happens to us as a result of what we have done. In this way he was able to show that risk is a function of what individuals do rather than of what »cultures« or »societies« do. It was this distinction that enabled me in my work on coping with disasters in southern Mozambique (Macamo 2017) to suggest that uncertainty may be an anthropological universal. If

---

**3** | The coup of 2014, which brought Mali's post Moussa Traoré's democratic experiment to an abrupt end and was staged by a junior army officer, is said to have benefitted from the support of young people.

that is indeed the case – and I suspect it is – we need to focus our attention on how it relates to social action.

I suggest that uncertainty bears on social life by turning social action into a self-reflexive activity. In other words, the reasons which individuals have to act do not necessarily yield the analytical rationality for which researchers are looking. The analytically relevant moment for the researcher is not how social actors achieve outcomes but rather how what they do enables them to act. To be more precise: we act in order to be able to act. (see Macamo 2017). The key insight here is not that outcomes do not matter – which of course they do. Yet, the focus on outcomes in the social sciences has prevented us from fully appreciating the extent to which processes matter. It is my contention that a greater focus on processes, as opposed to outcomes, may enable researchers to deal much better with the temporal dimension in their studies. One way of re-incorporating process into social analysis could be through paying greater attention to social situations.

As already suggested, social situations consist of the three parts referred to above, namely (a) interactional moments, (b) constitutive history, and (c) random factors. It is the failure to acknowledge the importance of process over outcome that renders us vulnerable to optimism and pessimism as basic analytical positions. In other words, we reduce our accounts of the social world to doing the right thing or celebrating the victimhood of social actors. Accounts become normative in ways which are not helpful in understanding the complexity of human social life.

## CAREER PATHS AND UNCERTAINTY

What are the implications of this to the project which lies at the heart of this volume? Our project was to explore the career paths of young graduates in Mali and Burkina Faso. The straightforward question that we asked was about what happens to them once they finish their studies. If we adhere to this straightforward question, we receive very straightforward and predictable answers. The optimist cannot help us; or rather, his or her answer is the kind of answer that would satisfy neither us nor our research subjects. In the best of all possible worlds – like the one which existed immediately after independence, when most countries were building up their »cadres« – anyone who studied well should be able to get a job upon completion of their studies. Conversely, those who did not get a job upon successful completion of their studies were unsuccessful because they were not good enough. The pessimist, by contrast, would not emphasise the individual to the same extent. Instead, he or she would say that structural conditions conspired to make it difficult for graduates to get a job upon finishing their studies.

Similarly to everything else in life, the answer is to be discovered in the middle and is not indicative of an either/or problem. Getting good grades is crucial, but even good grades will be useless if structural conditions are unfavourable. Favourable structural conditions, in turn, are likely to be a thing of the future, that is, invisible to the actor in the present. It is clear, then, that we need a more sophisticated question which places »uncertainty« at its centre. The question is not, therefore, »what happens to young graduates?« but rather how it is they deal with the basic uncertainty of transitioning from university to the job market. Hence, our research results addressed the three afore-mentioned parts of social situations.

In Burkina Faso, for example, Maike Birzle (see her contribution in this volume) focused on the interactional moment and found that »long bras«, i.e. the network of social relationships a graduate is able to muster for their job-seeking activity, was very important. In Mali, by contrast, Susann Ludwig's research (see her contribution in this volume) focused more on constitutive history and discovered that the ability to recognise opportunities when they arise was crucial – something she has termed »opening up *la chance*«.

The key issue, however, is that in both cases random factors are likely to play an inordinately large role, thus rocking the stability of constitutive histories and interactional moments. It is timely to seize this opportunity to explain the exact status of random factors, for they are important to our understanding of uncertainty.

Most social action takes place against the background of what phenomenologists describe as the natural attitude to the world (Schütz 1964; Schütz and Luckmann 1984; Berger and Luckmann 1991; Luhmann 1988). This is shaped by what is taken for granted, i.e. action does not consist in domesticating the unknown. Rather, it is shaped by dealing with familiar situations and applying known social recipes to them. The degree to which we are able to take most of our everyday life for granted also marks the degree to which most interaction is routine in our lives.

To the extent that interaction becomes routine we can also claim that constitutive histories and interactional moments are stable, by which we mean that social actors can formulate expectations and goals that are rendered intelligible and viable within the framework of the social situations in which they engage.

The taken-for-granted nature of social action is disrupted by problematic situations that require social actors to find ways of integrating them into the routines of their everyday lives. For example, if I went to an informal market in Bamako or Ouagadougou and discovered a non-negotiable price tag on every item, everything that I take for granted about going to the market in Bamako would be disrupted.[4] In fact, the claim that there are random factors means precisely this. Random factors are problematic situations in need of translation into normality. Social action becomes extremely difficult, yet not impossible, when random factors (i.e. problematic situations) become the norm to the point where the normal boundaries of social situations no longer pertain. When that is the case, interactional moments and constitutive histories become unstable. It is under these circumstances that uncertainty is heightened.

Let me digress here to highlight a general problem in the manner in which we deploy the vocabulary of social science to account for phenomena in Africa (see Macamo 2016a; Macamo 2016b). I suggest that the problem we face in undertaking to approach the African context is the problem of applying concepts developed in historically and socially different settings to account for local phenomena that are universally intelligible. Given the differences in economic, political and technological development, the use of such concepts tends to erase their constitutive history in favour of a focus on outcomes. When we apply them to Africa we place an emphasis on these outcomes and see the interactional moments as the simple deployment of prescriptive knowledge. Like this we fail to be sensitive to process. A good illustration of this point is the notion of democracy, for instance.

When we use this concept we take the relative success and stability of Western European countries as the yardstick against the background of which we judge the right experience of democracy. We see the setbacks

---

4 | It is common practice for these markets not to display the price of the items on sale; instead, prices are negotiated on the spot. The final price depends on the bargaining skills of both seller and buyer.

suffered by democracy in Mali, for example, as proof either of Malian culture's basic incompatibility with democracy or of the refusal of Malian politicians to be democratic. We do not acknowledge that setbacks can simply be a failure to correspond to an outcome, i.e. to the European situation obtaining at the moment. However, failure to correspond to an outcome says nothing about the possibility that the outcome might be achieved.

The reason why we do this is because we forget the history that led to the European outcome. In other words, we do not take into account the process behind the outcome. We neglect the fact that it took Europe several setbacks – including two World Wars, numerous civil wars, the horrors of fascism and communism, etc. – before the current democratic settlement could be achieved. Nevertheless, I hasten to add that acknowledging »process« does not imply that Mali needs to wait and see in order for it to become democratic one day. This is not the case, and the bad news is, sadly, that democracy may never come to Mali. This is what makes social life so fascinating even while it is so frustrating in its outcomes. It is also what makes the task of researching the future extremely difficult from a methodological point of view.

It follows that uncertainty is on the one hand a function of the relative weight of random factors and, on the other hand, of the instability of constitutive histories and interactional moments. Random factors usually determine the degree to which social action can be engaged with in a routine way. The less present they are, the more routine social action will be. The stronger they are, the more individuals must invest in placing themselves in a position to act. Outcomes, under conditions of uncertainty, recede into the background.

These hypotheses concerning the presence of random factors explain the difficulty of conducting research on objects with a strong future temporal dimension. Random factors are beyond the control of social actors. From an analytical point of view this means both that individuals have no solid basis upon which to purposefully direct their action with some degree of certainty of achieving their goals, and also that researchers' accounts are vulnerable to constant falsification due to the turn of events. »Elusive« futures in this sense refer to the basic uncertainty underlying social action.

## Conclusion

The research project on the career paths of young graduates in Mali and Burkina Faso brought to the fore a problem faced by the social sciences, namely the problem of producing descriptions of the social that can give individuals secure contexts within which they can formulate their goals. While it would be appealing to succeed in this endeavour, it seems more sensible to assume that such descriptions will remain hard to achieve. In fact, the purpose of this chapter has been to give an account of why such an endeavour is difficult. This account centres around the notion of uncertainty, which comes into full view through the methodological difficulty of foretelling the future.

The German sociologist Hans Joas has already drawn our attention to this difficulty in his discussion of the relevance of American Pragmatism to social theory (Joas 1996). He uses the notion of »ends in view« to give sociological substance to the invitation to look at the consequences of social action. His answer consists mainly in claiming that social action is creative, which I take to mean that it is always a new response to problems that may be old. In my own attempt at giving an account of this difficulty I have stressed the importance of focusing on the social situation, as suggested by Randall Collins (2014). Such a focus has the potential to retrieve the future as viable terrain for sociological research by enabling the researcher to develop ways of describing the manner in which social actors actually produce the context that both constrains and enables their action.

What makes the future elusive is not necessarily the inability of individuals to plan ahead with any certainty. Rather, it is the difficulty experienced by social researchers to produce meaningful descriptions of social reality that can enable social actors to formulate their goals with any degree of certainty. The morphology of uncertainty is key to the relevance of the social sciences in their role as accounts of social reality.

## BIBLIOGRAPHY

Beck, Ulrich. 1992. *Risk Society: Towards a New Modernity.* Thousand Oaks, London, New Delhi: Sage.

Beck, Ulrich, Anthony Giddens, Scott Lash. 1994. *Reflexive Modernization: Politics, Tradition and Aesthetics in the Modern Social Order.* Cambridge: Polity.

Berger, Peter, Thomas Luckmann. 1991. *The Social Construction of Reality: A Treatise in the Sociology of Knowledge.* London: Penguin.

Collins, Randall. 2014. *Interaction Ritual Chains.* Princeton: Princeton University Press.

Joas, Hans. 1996. *The Creativity of Action.* Chicago: Chicago University Press.

Luhmann, Niklas. 1993. *Risk: A Sociological Theory.* New York: De Gruyter.

Luhmann, Niklas. 1988. »Familiarity, Confidence, Trust.« In *Trust*, edited by Diego Gambetta. Oxford: Oxford University Press. 94-107.

Lupton, Deborah. 1999. *Risk.* London: Routledge.

Macamo, Elísio. 2017. *The Taming of Fate: Approaching Risk from a Social Action Perspective. Case Studies from Southern Mozambique.* CODESRIA: Dakar.

Macamo, Elísio. 2016a. »Words that Think for Us.« *Review of African Political Economy.* Retrieved 6 May, 2017. [http://roape.net/2016/12/07/blinded-capitalism-words-think-us]

Macamo, Elísio. 2016b. »Before We Start: Science and Power in the Constitution of Africa.« In *The Politics of Nature and Science in Southern Africa*, edited by Maano Ramutsindela, Giorgio Miescher, Melanie Boehi. Basel: Basler Afrika Bibliographien. 323-334.

Schütz, Alfred. 1964. »The Well-Informed Citizen. An Essay on the Social Distribution of Knowledge.« *Social Research* 13: 463-478.

Schütz, Alfred, Thomas Luckmann. 1984. *Strukturen der Lebenswelt.* Frankfurt am Main: Suhrkamp.

Stehr, Nico. 2001. *The Fragility of Modern Societies: Knowledge and Risk in the Information Age.* London: Sage.

© Zoumana Sidibé

© Salimata Sogodogo

# On the Authors

**Carole Ammann** holds a PhD in Social Anthropology. Her main concern is with questions of gender, gendered norms, statehood, transformations of the state, political participation, and everyday life. Further, she is interested in forms of governance and imageries of secondary cities in West Africa.

**Maike Birzle** is a social anthropologist who is currently working on her doctoral thesis on young graduates in Burkina Faso. She focuses on the role of hope in the context of academics' aspirations to an upward mobility that is often blocked in Burkina Faso. For this purpose she conducted ten months of field research in Ouagadougou and Bobo-Dioulasso.

**Michelle Engeler** holds a PhD in Social Anthropology and is currently a postdoctoral researcher at the Centre for African Studies Basel (CASB), University of Basel, Switzerland. Her research interests focus on the conjunction of people's life trajectories and political transformation processes in West Africa and include analyses of youth, intergenerational relations and mobility patterns of highly qualified people.

**Susann Ludwig** is a PhD student in African Studies and research assistant at the Centre for African Studies in Basel. Her current research focuses on academic youth in Mali, where she is interested in how they imagine and construct their futures while living and managing the present. She studied Social Anthropology (M.A.) at the Martin-Luther University in Halle-Wittenberg.

**Elísio Macamo** is Professor of Sociology and African Studies at the Department of Social Sciences, University of Basel.

**Joschka Philipps** is an SNF Postdoc Fellow from the Centre for African Studies Basel, currently based at the Université Sonfonia-Conakry in Guinea. The present contribution is part of his cumulative PhD dissertation, which explores the interdependencies between youth, protest movements and research methodologies in sub-Saharan Africa and beyond.

**Richard Faustine Sambaiga** holds a PhD in Social Anthropology and works as a lecturer at the Department of Sociology and Anthropology, University of Dar es Salaam in Tanzania. His research interests are in youth studies, social transformation, natural resource use and management, the social dimensions of governance, sexual and reproductive health, and social research and theory.

**Noemi Steuer** holds a PhD in Social Anthropology and works at the Centre for African Studies Basel (CASB), University of Basel, Switzerland. Her research interests include academic life-trajectories, social recognition and intergenerational relations. In addition, she is engaged in managing and scientifically consulting theatre and art projects in Switzerland, Germany and Mali.

**Julian Tadesse** is a sociologist with a focus on the Horn of Africa Region. He is a Research Fellow at the Zentrum Moderner Orient (ZMO) in Berlin and a PhD candidate at the University of Basel.

# Ethnologie und Kulturanthropologie

Martina Kleinert
**Weltumsegler**
Ethnographie eines mobilen Lebensstils zwischen Abenteuer, Ausstieg und Auswanderung

2015, 364 S., kart., zahlr. Abb.
29,99 € (DE), 978-3-8376-2882-1
E-Book
PDF: 26,99 € (DE), ISBN 978-3-8394-2882-5

Francis Müller
**Mit Behinderung in Angola leben**
Eine ethnografische Spurensuche in einer von Tretminen verletzten Gesellschaft

2016, 152 S., kart., zahlr. Abb.
24,99 € (DE), 978-3-8376-3480-8

Dieter Haller
**Tanger**
Der Hafen, die Geister, die Lust. Eine Ethnographie

2016, 356 S., kart., zahlr. Abb.
34,99 € (DE), 978-3-8376-3338-2
E-Book
PDF: 34,99 € (DE), ISBN 978-3-8394-3338-6

Leseproben, weitere Informationen und Bestellmöglichkeiten
finden Sie unter www.transcript-verlag.de

# Ethnologie und Kulturanthropologie

Marcus Andreas
**Vom neuen guten Leben**
Ethnographie eines Ökodorfes

2015, 306 S., kart., zahlr. Abb.
27,99 € (DE), 978-3-8376-2828-9
E-Book
PDF: 24,99 € (DE), ISBN 978-3-8394-2828-3

Jenny Schreiber
**Politics, Piety, and Biomedicine**
The Malaysian Transplant Venture

March 2017, 298 p., pb.
44,99 € (DE), 978-3-8376-3702-1
E-Book
PDF: 44,99 € (DE), ISBN 978-3-8394-3702-5

Thomas Stodulka
**Coming of Age on the Streets of Java**
Coping with Marginality, Stigma and Illness

January 2017, 286 p., pb., numerous partly col. ill.
39,99 € (DE), 978-3-8376-3608-6
E-Book
PDF: 39,99 € (DE), ISBN 978-3-8394-3608-0

**Leseproben, weitere Informationen und Bestellmöglichkeiten
finden Sie unter www.transcript-verlag.de**